7 Mindfulness Training Lessons

Improve Teammates' Ability to
Work as One with Right-Minded Thinking

Do No Harm.

Work As One.®

By
Dan Hogan
Certified Master Facilitator

Books by Dan Hogan

Reason, Ego, & the Right-Minded Teamwork Myth: *The Philosophy and Process for Creating a Right-Minded Team That Works Together as One*

Right-Minded Teamwork in Any Team: *The Ultimate Team Building Method to Create a Team That Works as One*

How to Facilitate Team Work Agreements: *A Practical, 10-Step Process for Building a Right-Minded Team That Works as One*

How to Apply the Right Choice Model: *Create a Right-Minded Team That Works as One*

7 Mindfulness Training Lessons: *Improve Teammates' Ability to Work as One with Right-Minded Thinking*

Right-Minded Teamwork: *9 Right Choices for Building a Team That Works as One*

Design a Right-Minded, Team-Building Workshop: *12 Steps to Create a Team That Works as One*

Achieve Your Organization's Strategic Plan: *Create a Right-Minded Team Management System to Ensure All Teams Work as One*

Copyright © 2022, 2025 by Dan Hogan, Lord & Hogan LLC. All rights reserved.

Contact Dan Hogan at Dan.Hogan@RightMindedTeamwork.com

This book is licensed for personal, non-commercial use only. No part of this publication may be reproduced, distributed, or transmitted in any form or by any means, including photocopying, recording, or other electronic or mechanical methods, without the prior written permission of the publisher, except for brief quotations embodied in critical reviews and certain other noncommercial uses permitted by copyright law.

ISBN: 978-1-939585-11-0

Acknowledgments & Appreciations

To the thousands of teammates, team leaders, and team-building facilitators with whom I've worked with over the last 40 years,

Thank You

For being my teacher.

Collectively, we created this awesome team-building program.

Right-Minded Teamwork is a business-oriented, psychological approach to team building where acceptance, forgiveness, and adjustment are teammate characteristics, and customer satisfaction is the team's result.

In addition, there are several special people I want to joyfully acknowledge and thank for their contributions.

First and foremost, I want to convey my deep and heartfelt gratitude to our editor, Erin Leigh. Thanks to her superb editing and vital guidance, Right-Minded Teamwork is now much easier to understand and successfully integrate into your team. Thank you, Erin. The RMT book series would not have happened without you.
(To contact Erin, email erin@thechoice.life.)

Next, a giant thank you to the Ebook Launch team. Dane Low, our book cover designer, created exceptional cover designs for the Right-Minded Teamwork book series. Thank you for elevating Right-Minded Teamwork. (To reach Dane visit EbookLaunch.com.)

Another sincere thank you goes out to Cathi Bosco, our graphic artist, who renovated and modernized many of our Right-Minded Teamwork process models, graphics, and illustrations
(reach her at CathiBosco.com).
And I also want to thank the Media A-Team, who created the original and current versions of the Right Choice Model
(find them at Mediaateam.com).

Finally, I want to express my gratitude to Jackie D'Elia, our website and UX designer, who successfully modernized the RightMindedTeamwork.com website into an easy-to-use platform. Her work allows us to share the RMT books, models, and other resources and materials with the world. Thank you, Jackie.
(Contact Jackie at JackieDElia.com.)

CONTENTS

Preface 13
The 7 Mindfulness Training Lessons 21
   The 7 Lessons: An Overview 21
   You Have Two Teachers: Reason & Ego 26
   You Have Only Two Response Choices 28
   You Are the Decision-Maker 29
   Trust Your Intuition as the Decision-Maker 31
   Right-Minded Teamwork Attitudes & Behaviors 40

The RMT Myth 57
   A Message from Reason 57
   The Myth 60
   Moral of the Story 65
   Reason's Personal Note to You 66

Applying the 7 Lessons 69
Acceptance 71
   Lesson #1 – I Am Not Upset 73
   Lesson #2 – I Accept 76

Forgiveness 79
   Lesson #3 – No Neutral Thought 81
   Lesson #4 – I Forgive 84
   Lesson #5 – I Transform 86

Adjustment 89
   Lesson #6 – I Adjust 91
   Lesson #7 – I Learn 93

Your New, Mindful Journey Begins 100

About the Author 103
   Books by Dan Hogan 106

Resources 110

Glossary of Right-Minded Teamwork Terms & Resources 111
   100% Customer Satisfaction 111
   7 Mindfulness Training Lessons 111
   10 Characteristics of Right-Minded Teammates 112
   12 Steps Workshop Design Process 113
   A Course in Miracles 113
   Accept, Forgive, Adjust 114
   Ally or Adversary Teammate 115
   Avoidance Behavior 116
   Battleground: Where People Are Punished for Mistakes 117
   Certified Master Facilitator (CMF) 118
   Classroom: Where People Learn from Mistakes 118
   Communication Work Agreement 119
   Create, Promote, Allow 120
   Critical Few: Complete Important Tasks First 120
   Decision-Maker: The Real You 121
   Decision-Maker: Trust Your Intuition 122
   Decision-Making Work Agreement 123

Desire & Willingness: Preconditions for Accountability 124
Do No Harm. Work as One. 125
Ego & Ego Attack 126
Interlocking Accountability 127
Moment of Reason 128
Onboarding New Teammates 128
Oneness vs. Separateness 129
Preventions & Interventions 130
Psychological Goals 131
Reason 132
Reason, Ego & the Right-Minded Teamwork Myth 133
Recognition: Make It Easy to Keep Going 134
Right Choice Model 135
Right-Minded Teamwork's 5-Element Framework 136
Right-Minded Teamwork's 5 Element Implementation Plan 137
Right-Minded Teamwork Attitudes & Behaviors 138
Right-Mindedness vs. Wrong-Mindedness 139
RMT Facilitator 140
Team Management System: An RMT Enterprise-Wide Process . 141
Team Operating System & Performance Factor Assessment 142
Thought System 143
Train Your Mind 144
Uncovering Root Cause 145
Unified Circle of Right-Minded Thinking 146
Work Agreements 147

7 Mindfulness Training Lessons

For Right-Minded Teamwork Thinking

1. I am not upset about this difficult team situation for the reason I think.

2. I accept and own my part in this situation.

3. It's impossible that my thoughts about this situation are neutral.

4. I forgive others and myself.

5. I will transform the effects of this difficult team situation.

6. I adjust my thinking and behavior.

7. I see every difficult team situation as a learning opportunity.

Preface

Welcome to Right-Minded Teamwork (RMT).

What is RMT?

Right-Minded Teamwork is an intelligent and empowering teamwork system that creates a *team that works together as one.*

Every one of us has the right to experience the magic that can happen when teammates work together as *one unified team*. Each of us can claim and exercise that right, starting right now, if we choose. That is why RMT is for everyone, everywhere, forever. And, through these pages, it is available to you.

Apply RMT, and you will improve your work processes and strengthen your relationships.

Apply RMT, and your team will achieve 100% customer satisfaction.

Apply RMT, and your team will *work together as one.*

You'll also do your part to make the world a better place for everyone, everywhere, forever.

. . . . .

Welcome! It is an honor to introduce you to Right-Minded Teamwork and RMT's *7 Mindfulness Training Lessons*.

RMT is a unique, real-world, continuous improvement method that has improved the lives and teams of thousands of people worldwide. Apply RMT processes and these Lessons in your team, and you, too, will reap the benefits.

Before we get started, let's answer a few questions that may be on your mind.

Is This Book for You?

Do you desire a world...

That you rule instead of one that rules you?
Where you are powerful instead of helpless?
In which you have no adversaries, only allies?

Are you ready to live in the beautiful world offered to you by Reason, instead of feeling lost and alone thanks to Ego?

If you answered yes to these questions, the 7 Mindfulness Training Lessons will help you achieve your goals.

These Lessons can be summed up in one sentence, with emphasis on three words:

*Right-Minded Teammates **accept**, **forgive**, and **adjust** their thinking and work behavior.*

What Is This Book About?

In every circumstance, and especially during difficult team situations, Right-Minded Teammates practice **mindfulness** to move into a Right-Minded, ally-focused way of thinking, seeing, and behaving.

Mindfulness is your conscious ability to monitor your thoughts in the present. At the same time, you calmly acknowledge and accept your thoughts, feelings, and behaviors and those of others.

Your quiet mindfulness in the face of conflict is the catalyst for experiencing a **moment of Reason**.

In a moment of Reason, the best way to respond to a challenging team situation becomes instantly clear. Reason allows appropriate, Right-Minded attitudes and behaviors to surface easily and automatically in your mind.

By applying these 7 Mindfulness Training Lessons, you, along with Reason's help, will shift your perspective. You will learn how to ensure you always respond in the best way possible to challenging team situations and circumstances.

Who Are Reason & Ego?

In the RMT book Reason, Ego & the *Right-Minded Teamwork Myth: The Philosophy and Process for Creating a Right-Minded Team That Works Together as One,* a short, simple story reveals the experiences of three characters: Reason, Ego, and you, the Decision-Maker.

Simply summarized, the story advocates that teammates apply Reason's guidance and seek Oneness and shared interest over Ego's disastrous advice to pursue separateness and selfishness. This story illustrates the Right-Minded Teamwork philosophy and demonstrates a Right-Minded way of thinking, seeing, and behaving.

You will also find this story, called the *Right-Minded Teamwork Myth*, later in this book.

Where Did These Lessons Come From?

Over the course of my 40-year career in team building and facilitation, I had the honor of working with hundreds of teams and thousands of beautifully diverse people all around the world. As much as I was hired to help them, they also taught me lessons, including the ones found on these pages.

In other words, these 7 Lessons came from people just like you.

I like to believe these Lessons are universal and have been available to all of us since the beginning of time (of course, whether we choose to use them is a different question altogether!). Additionally, the concepts we'll discuss here are pulled from two sources: *A Course in Miracles*, and Right-Minded Teamwork's Right Choice Model.

For more about *A Course in Miracles*, go to FACIM.org.

We will review RMT's Right Choice Model later in this book, but for a more in-depth exploration, check out the RMT book **How to Apply the Right Choice Model**: *Create a Right-Minded Team That Works as One,* available at RightMindedTeamwork.com or your favorite book retailer.

How Do These 7 Lessons Address Team Issues?

When difficult team situations occur, and you and your teammates practice the 7 Lessons, you shift your perspective and consistently **accept, forgive**, and **adjust** your collective attitudes and behaviors. Your real-time adjustment allows you to respond and recover from challenging team situations successfully. Most importantly, you actually resolve your team's problems.

It is truly that simple. For this reason, I pray that mindfulness lessons will one day become a prevailing team-building approach around the world.

I'm optimistic it will happen. I genuinely believe that as more people like you understand and embrace mindfulness to create better, stronger teams, we will see less and less of those old, ineffective, and often silly approaches to team-building.

I also believe in a better future for teams because I know I'm not alone in wanting it. For decades, my clients have expressed the same desire. They were changed by our work together, what they learned, and how Right-Minded Teamwork helped them achieve team goals.

With them, the ripple effect began. Through you, it will continue. Together, we will build better teams - teams that **do no harm** and **work as one**.

Welcome to Your New Role: RMT Leader & Facilitator

Now that you have a clearer sense of the journey we'll be taking together through these pages, I want to take a moment to congratulate you on your new role. Incorporating the 7 Mindful Training Lessons into your team-building repertoire means **you are now a Right-Minded Teamwork leader and facilitator.**

As an RMT leader and facilitator, **your specialty is team transformations.**

Using RMT, you help to transform dysfunctional souls into healthy and functional teammates. You guide teammates to convert their mistakes into Right-Minded attitudes and behaviors. They express their deep and heartfelt gratitude for your facilitation efforts and results. Some even say you "saved them," continuing to seek your support for years to come.

All parts of Right-Minded Teamwork, including the 7 Mindfulness Training Lessons, Right Choice, and team Work Agreements, are available for your use. There are no licensing or certification requirements.

As you continue your RMT journey, my only request is that you accept Reason's wisdom on this path. With Reason's guidance, you can easily apply these methods to help your teams create and sustain Right-Minded Teamwork.

My Special Support Function

It took countless workshops, a 35-year career in active team-building facilitation, and the collective wisdom of so many teammates and team leaders to conceptualize and build Right-Minded Teamwork into the robust model it is today.

Though I no longer facilitate actively, choosing to pass that torch on to the next generation of leaders and facilitators, I will always continue to promote Right-Minded Teamwork.

The reason for my continued passion is quite simple. I know, beyond a shadow of a doubt, that RMT's methods, including the 7 Mindfulness Training Lessons are right for every team, everywhere, forever. If you use them, they will help make your client team(s) and the world a better place.

To make that happen, though, **your team needs you to show them the Right-Minded Teamwork way.**

As you lead them down the RMT path, remember: I am here to support you. So, reach out to me. Ask me questions. Let me get to know you so I can refer you to clients looking for an RMT leader or facilitator.

Also remember that even though you will undoubtedly help your teams achieve an "early win," creating and sustaining Right-Minded Teamwork takes at least a year.

So, as you enter into the team-building process, stick with it for the long haul. Plan to stay with your team(s) for at least one to two years. Help them firmly establish RMT in their team. Give them the foundation they need to learn, grow, and succeed.

As you do, you will do *your part to make the world a better place for everyone, everywhere, forever.*

Now, let's get started.

Dan Hogan

PS - Here's a quick preview. In the coming pages, I will introduce you to the 7 Mindfulness Training Lessons and several other important mindful concepts. After that, you will find the delightful Right-Minded Teamwork Myth, along with an encouraging message to you from Reason. Lastly, you will learn how to apply these Lessons in your life.

Ready? Let's go!

The 7 Mindfulness Training Lessons

Mindfulness is your conscious ability to monitor your thoughts in the present. When you are mindful, you calmly acknowledge and accept your thoughts, feelings, and behaviors, as well as those of others.

Your calm mindfulness is the necessary condition for shifting your perspective to experience a **moment of Reason**, which is the precursor to finding real teamwork solutions.

When you practice mindfulness by following these 7 Lessons, you also put into practice the Right-Minded attitudes and behaviors taught to you in the Right Choice Model.

The 7 Lessons: An Overview

1. I am not upset about this difficult situation for the reason I think.

2. I **accept** and own my part in this situation.

3. It's impossible that my thoughts about this situation are neutral.

4. I **forgive** others and myself.

5. I will transform the effects of this difficult team situation.

6. I **adjust** my thinking and behavior.

7. I see every difficult team situation as a learning opportunity.

In every circumstance, especially during difficult team situations, Right-Minded Teammates use these Lessons to practice mindfulness to move them into a Right-Minded, "we are allies" way of thinking and behaving.

These Lessons are effective. Apply them, and you, along with Reason's help, will find the best way to respond in all situations and circumstances.

Applying the Lessons: Self-Study or Team Study

There are two options for applying the 7 Mindfulness Lessons: self-study or team study. Both are recommended.

If you are pursuing **team study**, be sure to provide teammates with the 7 Lessons cards and posters, available for download at RightMindedTeamwork.com.

When you opt for a team approach, in addition to this book, you will want to consult the book ***Right-Minded Teamwork in Any Team***: *The Ultimate Team-Building Method to Create a Team That Works as One.*

There, you will discover a three-workshop implementation plan. If you choose to follow the plan, the third workshop, focused on Right-Minded Teammate development, is a wonderful time to explore and discuss how the 7 Mindfulness Training Lessons may be applied in your team.

If you are pursuing **self-study**, in the Applying the 7 Lessons section of this book, you will learn how to use the Lessons to transform a difficult situation you likely know very well: the Constantly Complaining Teammate (CCT).

Having a Constantly Complaining Teammate on your team may be the reason you are seeking teamwork solutions.

Though a CCT's complaints may look or sound different day to day or from team to team, a similar message usually underpins their efforts.

They typically insist,

> *My life can't get better until you change.*

They believe they are right. They think you and everyone else are wrong. That is why they believe you must change.

Fortunately, the challenge of the CCT can be addressed by applying the 7 Mindfulness Lessons. This book will show you how. Once you understand how to apply these 7 Lessons with a CCT, you will know how to do the same in all your difficult situations.

7 Lessons: A Testimonial

While working on this book series, I received a note from a Right-Minded teammate who had actively applied the 7 Lessons to transform a challenging situation. She shared:

> *Recently, I was reflecting on a challenging situation with a fellow entrepreneur (not my "team," per se, but within my circle of influence). As I was trying to figure out how I wanted to approach it, the first of the 7 Lessons of Right-Minded Thinking popped into my mind.*
>
> ***"I am not upset about this difficult team situation for the reason I think,"*** *I told myself. Immediately I could see there was more to the situation than just the surface-level issue. No wonder it felt so heavy and complicated.*
>
> *Seeing as I'd already made progress, I figured I might as well apply the next few Mindfulness Lessons, too. As I did, I could feel myself relaxing, and, in just a few moments, I was able to see the situation completely differently.*
>
> *My inner resistance has dissipated, and therefore the issue has, too. I had no doubt your methodology was effective, but I didn't realize how immediately transformative it could be.*
>
> *Thank you and RMT for this personal breakthrough!*

Why Use the 7 Mindful Lessons?

Whether you are aware of it or not, your thoughts determine how you behave. Your thought system produces choices and behaviors. Those decisions either transform you and your teammates into classmates and allies or prisoners and adversaries.

If you dread working with your teammates or your customers, you are in a psychological prison. You don't want to be in prison. No one wants you there.

The 7 Lessons can get you out of prison. They are the way to freedom.

If you don't dread working with your teammates, these Lessons are still relevant. They will strengthen your ability to collaborate and make better team decisions.

Your desire to improve your situation is your motivation to apply these Lessons in your daily work life. You can apply the Lessons anytime, but they are especially useful when you experience disagreements and conflicts.

They have the power to transform any circumstance or event into a wonderful learning opportunity, making every day an exciting new adventure in the classroom of life.

In this classroom, you have two teachers or two thought systems. Let us introduce them. Then, we will dive into the 7 Lessons and how to apply them.

You Have Two Teachers: Reason & Ego

Reason and Ego are your teachers. They live inside your mind.

They teach you the Decision-Maker, how to think, see, and behave.

If you choose to follow Reason, you'll learn how to use the 7 Lessons to create a wonderful classroom with enjoyable classmates. Reason will teach you how to get and stay in your Right Mind.

If you choose to follow Ego's advice, your behavior will keep you in jail. Ego distracts you and keeps you from your Right Mind.

Ego is a negative influence who believes your team is much like a prison. Ego is constantly talking inside your head, urgently telling you it's a desperate world out there. People are out to get you, Ego reminds. Ego tells you it's everyone else's fault (not yours!) that you are stuck where you are, suffering within your team.

Ego is a noisy, wrong-minded teacher; it teaches you to attack and blame. And if you don't listen to Ego and do what you've been told, Ego attacks and blames you for not following its advice.

Reason, on the other hand, is your calm, Right-Minded teacher.

Reason asks you to see your team environment as a wonderful and safe classroom. Reason knows and consistently reminds you that you and your teammates will be much better off working together as one unified team.

To achieve that unity, Reason will gladly show you how to apply these 7 Lessons. They guarantee you will create a Right-Minded Teamwork classroom where everyone learns and benefits.

You Have Only Two Response Choices

The Right-Minded Teamwork philosophy teaches that you are the **Decision-Maker**, and you only have two choices regarding how you respond to every difficult situation.

When a challenging situation happens, you either:
- accept Ego's guidance and act like a victim or victimizer, or
- embrace Reason and act in an accountable, Right-Minded way.

Even though there are many variations of those two choices, *there are still just two.*

At all times, you are mindful, or you are mindless. You are either following your Right Mind, Reason, or your wrong mind, Ego. You see other's Ego behaviors as attacks, or you change your perspective and interpret their behavior as a call for your help.

For the background story behind the *RMT's 7 Mindful Training Lessons*, read RMT's *Reason, Ego, and the Right-Minded Teamwork Myth* later in this book. This story introduces the three characters who live in every teammate's life.

You Are the Decision-Maker

The RMT philosophy plus the Right Choice Model says "you" are your own internal Decision-Maker.

This "you" is your observer, interpreter, and decider. It is the part of you that sees all your experiences and determines how you will respond to those situations.

Look closely at the Right Choice Model now.

Do you see yourself, the Decision-Maker, sitting right in the middle between your difficult situation and the choice you must make?

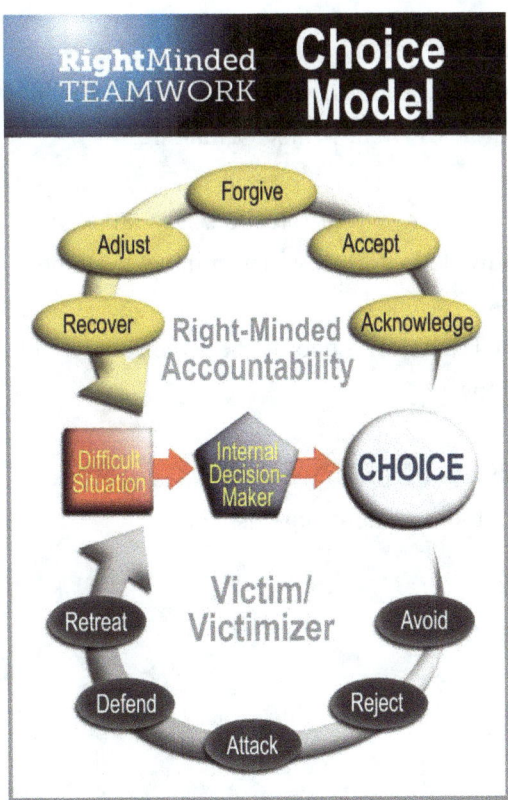

In this position, between the difficult situation you are facing and the choice you must make, you are faced with two choices. You either choose the right direction – as described in the 7 Lessons – or the wrong direction.

As the Decision-Maker, you are never alone during these moments of choice.

Reason and Ego are always there in your mind, every time you make choices, whether you are conscious of them or not. Each time you make a decision, you either mindfully and consciously choose to follow your team's Work Agreements and the 7 Mindful Lessons, or you mindlessly and unconsciously decide to follow Ego's tragic wrong-minded thinking.

Applying the 7 Lessons plus choosing the upper loop means **accepting**, **forgiving**, and **adjusting**, which is your mindful move into the Unified Circle of Right-Minded Thinking.

In contrast, the lower loop of rejection, Ego attack, and defensiveness describes the divided circle of wrong-minded thinking.

Right-Minded Teamwork upholds the upper circle and the 7 Mindful Training Lessons.

For more about Right-Minded attitudes, see the Right-Minded Teamwork Attitudes & Behaviors list below.

Trust Your Intuition as the Decision-Maker

If thinking about Reason and Ego is new to you, it can be helpful to think of Reason as your positive intuition and Ego as your negative, arrogant, and sometimes vindictive intuition.

At different times throughout our lives, we all listen to and follow each of these teachers.

Stop and remember when you had a hunch or feeling about what you should do or say in a particular situation. Did you ignore your intuition? Let's say you did not follow your instinct, and it turned out to be a mistake. What did you say to yourself and others?

> *I wish I had trusted my intuition!*

As this memory illustrates, **you already know how to listen and be mindful** of your intuition. It is your natural pre-separation state of mind. You just need to do it regularly.

If not…

Remember a time when you became angry, agitated, or annoyed with a teammate. Without thinking, you said mean-spirited things. You, too, were saying to yourself, *"My life can't get better until you change."* Accept it. Your negative behavior happened because you did not stop for a **moment of Reason**.

You were literally *out of your Right Mind* as you unconsciously turned towards Ego for guidance.

During your reaction, you were mindless as you followed Ego's advice. Then, after a while, once you stepped back and calmed down, you could see your behavior was a mistake - only a mistake, to be corrected, not punished. At this moment, you shifted your perspective. You forgave yourself, and you adjusted by apologizing and promising not to behave that way again. You returned to your Right Mind.

If you are not accustomed to trusting your intuition but would like to do so more, you will need to practice.

> *The key is to **pause** and be **still**. Remember Lesson 1 – you are not upset for the reason you think, which is the catalyst for shifting perspectives. Now, intentionally **listen** for your positive intuition - that **moment of Reason** before you react to a situation or event.*

It is that simple. But that does not make it easy, especially at first. It takes mindful practice to *train your mind* to listen for this joyous, intuitive moment. It takes an unwavering commitment to stop yourself continually, gently, and compassionately when you become angry, fearful, agitated, or anxious.

It is not always easy, but it can be done. Many have learned this skill. You can, too. As the Decision-Maker, you always have free will regarding whether you choose to follow Ego or Reason. Even if you've tried before and failed, you can start again today.

Remember that even with steadfast commitment, it will take practice to excel. You will make mistakes. That's okay. Choose Reason again. Choose to apply these 7 Lessons and to follow your Work Agreements again. And again, and again. When you realize you've chosen Ego, apologize, forgive, correct, forget the mistake and move on. The more you practice, the easier it will get.

You will soon find that as you change your mind, you automatically change your behavior. And when you change your behavior, you transform your team into a lovely learning classroom. The more you make an effort to *be* **in your Right Mind**, the easier it will become to *stay* **in your Right Mind**.

Now, instead of saying, *"I wish I had listened to my intuition,"* you will say,

> *I'm so glad I* **turned towards** *Reason and followed my intuition!*

EGO

DECISION MAKER

REASON

Mindfulness *Is* Choice in Action

When you are mindless, you don't think or reflect. Instead of *consciously* choosing how to respond, you react *unconsciously* in an emotionally immature way, blaming others or avoiding the situation altogether.

When you're mindful, you reflect and carefully choose how you respond to everything that happens to you and around you. When a difficult situation occurs, being mindful means first remembering Lesson 1:

> *I'm not upset for the reason I think.*

This is the first step in changing perspective. Secondly, ask yourself this question, which is a key part of the Right Choice Model:

> *What did I do or say to **create**, **promote**, or **allow** this to happen?*

Your answers to this question help you and your team experience a **moment of Reason**, which paves the way for you to create real solutions.

As an example, let's assume a significant mistake has happened in your team.

Half the team is aggressively blaming the other half for the mistake in what is often called an **"Ego attack."**

> **RIGHT-MINDED Accountability**
>
> is the **desire, willingness, and ability** to change my mind & behavior in order to effectively respond to difficult situations.
>
> **This means owning my part in the situation by asking:**
>
> *"How did I CREATE, PROMOTE, or ALLOW this difficult situation to happen?"*
>
> RightMindedTeamwork.com

Teammates are making toxic and hurtful statements, directly and indirectly, about each other. The team is stuck in a battleground of "attack and defend." No one is working to resolve the mistake.

Seeking a **moment of Reason**, you ask yourself,

> *What am I doing to create, promote, or allow this blaming conversation to continue?*

You realize you've been standing by and saying nothing. You were **avoiding**, which is the **first step in the lower loop** of the Right Choice Model.

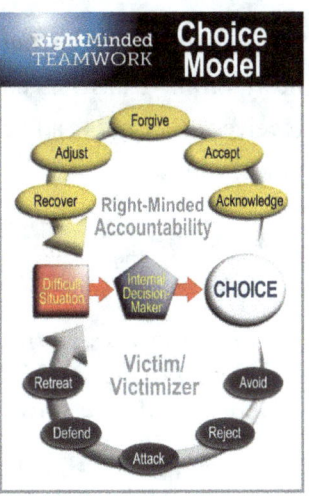

Now that you are aware of your attitude and behavior, you desire to change your mind. You remember the 7 Lessons, and you begin stating them in your Right Mind. Your "remembering" is your choice to follow Reason and act in a Right-Minded, accountable way, just as your Work Agreement states.

Reason is that part of your mind that always speaks for the Right Choice attitudes and behaviors. When you are facing a difficult team situation and need a **moment of Reason**, to find the best way to respond to a difficult team situation, say to yourself:

> *I am here to be truly helpful.*
>
> *I am here to represent Reason who sent me.*
>
> *I do not have to worry about what to say or what to do because Reason who sent me will direct me.*

As you pause, you are able to remember two Right-Minded responses, both of which are likely part of your Work Agreements:
- Engage in helpful problem-solving communication.
- Correct mistakes rather than punish and blame.

As you reflect while holding these two choices in your mind and heart, *intuitive* answers come to your "right" mind. Now that you have received Reason's advice, in a calm, "do-no-harm-work-as-one" voice, you say,

> *Here's a suggestion. Let's discuss what we know, the facts, about what happened. Then let's find an immediate solution.*
>
> *After we resolve the mistake, let's have a second team discussion, not to blame, but to create a Work Agreement so that this mistake doesn't happen again. How does that sound?*

If you had followed Ego's advice and continued your **avoidance behavior**, the conflict would have continued.

Since you chose to look towards Reason, you created an environment where you and your teammates **recovered** from the mistake, the **last step in the upper loop** of the model.

Reason's 7 Mindful Lessons, as always, have brought you - and hopefully everyone else, too - **back into your Right Mind.**

By listening to Reason, trusting your intuition, changing your perspective, and following the 7 Lessons and your Work Agreements, you are successfully training your mind to consistently return to the Unified Circle of Right-Minded Thinking.

Return to the Unified Circle of Right-Minded Thinking

When your team discusses and agrees on your psychological goals – your consciously chosen set of attitudes and behaviors as described in your Work Agreements – you have created your team's collective thought system.

By uniting with each other in this way and openly committing to one another through your Work Agreements, you are renouncing Ego in yourself and your teammates and collectively committing to train your minds to follow Reason.

This process of creating team Work Agreements is your undivided declaration of interdependence. Your assertion is saying,

> *We hold these mindful truths to be self-evident that all minds are created equal, and whosoever believes that will have everlasting freedom to choose Right-Minded teamwork.*

Your declaration, combined with the daily acts of living your team Work Agreements, form your return to the forgiving Unified Circle of Right-Minded Thinking.

The one fundamental freedom no one can take away from you is your *freedom to choose* how to respond to life's challenges.

At every moment, your Decision-Maker is making that choice in one of two ways: Either your Decision-Maker is choosing based on Ego's wrong-minded dictates or Reason's Right-Minded principles and your team's Work Agreements.

> *Follow Reason, and you declare your freedom from Ego's battlefields.*
>
> *Follow Reason, and you have joined others who hold these Right-Minded thoughts to be self-evident and true.*
>
> *Follow Reason, and you transform your fixed perspectives by reinterpreting attack behaviors as a call for help – your help.*
>
> *Follow Reason, and your team will agree on a Right-Minded set of attitudes and behaviors as described in your* **Work Agreements.**
>
> *By following* **Reason** *and your* **Work Agreements**, *you will renounce Ego while uniting with your fellow teammates.*
>
> *You will return to your ultimate goal, the forgiving Unified Circle of Right-Minded Thinking.*

What Is "Right" in Right-Minded Teamwork?

RMT has nothing to do with right-brain thinking or right-wing viewpoints.

It has everything to do with what your team, together, decides is "right." Your team's choices, identified collectively, define your team's Right-Minded attitudes and work behaviors.

*The "right" way is the way you **choose** is right for your team.*

So, how do you open up a team discussion about what is right or wrong for your team?

One of the best ways is to introduce the Right Choice Model to your team and ask if all teammates will actively live your team's Right-Minded Teamwork attitudes and behaviors. A team discussion on the attitudes and behaviors presented on the following pages can then follow.

Right-Minded Teamwork Attitudes & Behaviors

Over decades of team-building work, I worked with hundreds of teams. Along the way, I collected their Right-Minded attitudes and behaviors into a list of choices that I grouped into **work behaviors** and **work processes**. Use this list to either adopt or adapt as your team's Psychological Goals and Work Agreements.

Were You Born with These Thoughts & Attitudes?

Thoughts and attitudes always precede teamwork behavior.

Right-Minded attitudes and these 7 Mindful Training Lessons come from Reason. Wrong-minded attitudes come from Ego.

The good news is that Right-Minded attitudes and these Lessons are natural. They are already inside you and your teammates.

When you think about any of the wrong-minded Ego attitudes listed below, ask yourself,

> *Was I born with these depressing, debilitating, and awful attitudes?*

Your answer will always be **"no!"**

You learned those wrong-minded attitudes from Ego. That means *you can unlearn them, too.* And the 7 Mindful Training Lessons *is how you unlearn them!*

You Can Change Your Mind

In 35 years of team-building facilitation, I heard too many well-intentioned albeit wrong-minded teammates say,

> *That's just the way I am. I can't change.*

That is **simply not true**.

What is true is that they refused to change their minds.

> *When someone says they cannot change, what they are really saying is their behavior is more powerful than their mind.*

When you realize and joyfully accept that **your mind is in charge**, you open the way for happiness, inner peace, and Right-Minded Teamwork *Thinking*.

Why You Want to Change Your Perspective

Fixed perspectives prevent you from achieving Right-Minded Thinking. Your fixed beliefs, interpretations, and perspectives are blocks to Right-Minded Thinking.

To remove those blocks, you must want to transform those thoughts.

You can start with Lesson 1 of the 7 Lessons, which states, "I am never upset for the reason I think." This first lesson invites a **moment of Reason.**

By applying Lesson 1 when a difficult team situation occurs, instead of seeing your teammate's behavior as a negative Ego attack, you are able to reinterpret their behavior as a desperate **call for help**.

With just the first Lesson, you have changed your perspective.

On the next page, you will find a list of 30 Right-Minded Teamwork Attitudes & Behaviors that will help you change your perspective, choose Reason over Ego, and achieve Right-Minded Thinking.

Work Behavior Attitudes

As the Decision-Maker, You Behave One Way or the Other!

EGO — DECISION MAKER — REASON

Demonstrate adversarial competition and power struggles	Demonstrate collaborative competition and synergy
Demonstrate victim or victimizer attitudes & behaviors	Exhibit accountable and responsible attitudes & behavior
Worry that "I am my mistakes;" continue to obsess over mistakes	Embrace that "I am not my mistakes;" mistakes are opportunities for me to learn
Noticeable lack of emotional maturity and empathy	Desire to be emotionally mature and compassionate
Exhibit self-centered attitudes	Exhibit we-centered attitudes
Hold & project grievances; Never forget or forgive	Embrace & extend forgiveness; Let go of issues from the past
After mistakes, helplessness occurs, and I choose to give up or not try as hard	After mistakes, forgiveness occurs, and I choose to try again and again

Work Behavior Attitudes (Continued)

There's a mindset of scarcity, a belief that to give is to lose	There's an attitude of abundance, a belief that to give is to receive
There is suspicion, closed-mindedness, and resistance to change	There is readiness and open-mindedness for positive change
Too often, people restate their position, believing they are right, and others are wrong	We always seek mutual understanding: believing together, we are right
I believe I'm the smartest, and I can prove it	We believe none of us is as smart as all of us
I demonstrate a conscious or unconscious attitude of confusion, chaos, complexity, and drama	We continually demonstrate a conscious attitude of clarity, order, simplicity, and calmness
There's a widespread belief that difficult team situations and changes determine how we feel	We know for sure that our minds determine how we feel about difficult situations or changes
We believe it is best to keep quiet when correction is needed	We have a team culture of appropriately speaking up when a correction is needed
We believe in these attitudes: vulnerability, unkindness, hate, attack, blame	We embrace these attitudes: invulnerability, love, kindness, do no harm, work as one

Work Behavior Attitudes (Continued)

We believe in power over others	We believe in power with others
Growth is painful; remember, if there is no pain, there is no gain	Growth doesn't have to be painful; learning is joyously attained and gladly remembered
It is best to do unto others (reject, attack, defend) before they do unto you	We do unto others (accept, forgive, adjust) as we would have them do unto us
There is a feeling of avoidance and criticism among teammates	There is a spirit of acknowledgment and reward among teammates
There is a love and a need for power, fame, money, and pleasure	We strive for non-attachment to power, fame, money, and pleasure
Our team is a battleground where conflict is prolonged as we act like victims or victimizers	Our team is our learning classroom where conflict is resolved as we act like Right-Minded Teammates
There is mistrust, fear, and lack of safety among teammates	There is trust, peace, and safety among teammates
Defensiveness is prevalent in our team	Defenselessness is widespread in our team

Process Behavior Attitudes

Your Team Can Operate One Way or the Other!

The team's purpose, vision, and mission are unclear and not supported	Our team continuously clarifies our purpose, vision, and mission and actively supports them
There is no discernable team operating system	There is an efficient, continuous improvement team operating system in place
There is a predominant attitude of avoidance and complaining	We have an attitude and a system for acknowledgment and reward
Disagreements and a lack of clear roles and responsibilities exist	We periodically clarify teammate roles and responsibilities
We are unclear who makes decisions and how	Our team has a clear and effective decision-making Work Agreement
We spend too much time and energy applying inefficient work processes	Our work processes and procedures are clear, understood, accepted, and efficient
Too often, people are punished for making mistakes	We always embrace an attitude of converting mistakes into learning opportunities

Actionable Attitudes = Better Behaviors

These Right-Minded attitudes are practical. However, these noble thoughts and attitudes will do no good unless you discuss them and define what they mean for your team.

Once you have identified and defined the behaviors associated with your chosen attitudes, captured in your team Work Agreements, you must also make the conscious choice to live them going forward.

Don't let your team's insignificant, Ego-driven squabbles pull you down.

Be vigilant and demonstrate by your actions and behaviors that you have risen above your old, petty, teamwork battleground issues.

No team situation can pull you into Ego's realm of conflict when you believe it is far better to collaborate and win than argue and lose.

Remember, it is from your collective Right Mind that you create your Work Agreements. And when you make and follow your promises, you are uniting with each other without the Ego. When you do that, you have returned to the United Circle of Right-Minded Thinking. From that unified circle, it will be much easier to recover from any difficult team situation because you have, at that moment, restored your team's collective Right Mind to Reason.

The 10 Characteristics of Right-Minded Teammates

Right-Minded Teammates have diverse backgrounds, vastly different experiences, and display a wide range of skills. No two are alike. Still, there are certain characteristics all Right-Minded Teammates share.

These characteristics align the teammate's authentic self with the RMT motto of *Do no harm and work as one*. They are:

1. Trust
2. Honesty
3. Tolerance
4. Gentleness
5. Joy
6. Defenselessness
7. Generosity
8. Patience
9. Open-mindedness
10. Faithfulness

When you help your team create and live team Work Agreements, they will be well on their way to living these characteristics.

How does the Right-Minded Teammate live these characteristics?

They do two things when difficult situations occur.

First, they remind themselves of their commitment to *thinking* in a do-no-harm way. Second, they choose to demonstrate do-no-harm *behaviors* that align with their Right-Minded attitudes, such as finding solutions to challenging situations.

It is not always easy to do these two things, but it is always that simple.

To encourage your team to embrace and live these Right-Minded characteristics, check out these two RMT books:

7 Mindfulness Training Lessons: Improve Teammates' Ability to Work as One with Right-Minded Thinking will teach you how to apply RMT's seven, powerful thinking lessons to encourage Right-Minded, unified teamwork.

How to Apply the Right Choice Model: Create a Right-Minded Team That Works as One teaches you how to transform a disappointed team customer into a 100% satisfied customer by making Right-Minded choices, all of which align with the above list of characteristics.

For now, though, let's take a closer look at each of these 10, Right-Minded Teammate characteristics.

1. Trust

Trust is the foundational characteristic for teammates who desire to create and sustain Right-Minded Teamwork. Right-Minded Teammates trust one another because their own past experience has taught them that, in all situations, a forgiving attitude creates safety for teammates to collaborate and resolve difficulties.

2. Honesty

For the Right-Minded Teammate, honesty means more than just telling the truth. It refers to consistency in thought and deed. An honest, Right-Minded Teammate is consistently looking within and striving to align thoughts, words, and behaviors with the team's psychological goals and forgiving values. This kind of honesty is essential to creating and sustaining Right-Minded Teamwork.

3. Tolerance

Judgment is the opposite of forgiveness; it implies a lack of trust. Tolerance indicates non-judgment. Tolerant teammates do not judge one another because they know that though they are not the same, all Right-Minded Teammates are equal. Their tolerance creates space for the wisdom of diversity to surface, and their equality allows them to work together as one.

4. Gentleness

Right-Minded Teammates believe that gentleness is the only sane response to challenging situations and circumstances. Whereas harshness and judgment close doors, gentleness opens them. With gentleness, it is easy for teammates to do no harm as they work as one – with teammates and customers alike.

5. Joy

Joy is the inevitable result of Right-Minded teammates who are gentle and non-judgmental. Fear is impossible for those who are gentle, especially during challenging situations. Joy comes from gentleness, tolerance, honesty, and forgiveness.

6. Defenselessness

Right-Minded Teammates understand that defenses are foolish, judgmental attitudes and behaviors that prevent the team from finding solutions to difficult situations. When teammates summon the courage to forgive and trust themselves and to look honestly at their wrong-minded defenses without judgment, they can lay those debilitating arguments gently aside, creating the proper conditions for honestly doing no harm and working as one.

7. Generosity

Right-Minded Teammates honestly and humbly give all they know to help their team create Right-Minded Teamwork and achieve 100% customer satisfaction. The world teaches that if you give something away, you lose it, but Right-Minded Teammates realize that to give *is* to receive. They eagerly participate with their teammates to create solutions to solve challenging situations, bringing joy and satisfaction to the team through their gentle generosity.

8. Patience

Teammates who know Right-Minded Teamwork is the outcome they want can easily afford to wait without concern. Because their goal is to be tolerant and gentle with their teammates, patience comes naturally. The highest desire is to work as one.

9. Open-Mindedness

Judgment, or wrong-mindedness, closes teammates' minds, creating resistance to Right-Minded Teamwork. To ensure they do no harm while working as one, Right-Minded Teammates embrace open-mindedness, also known as Right-Mindedness.

10. Faithfulness

Faithfulness describes a teammate's trust in their team's version of Right-Minded Teamwork. When a teammate is faithful, they effortlessly and wholeheartedly believe in Right-Minded Teamwork. They *want* to do no harm and work as one. They know none of us is as smart as all of us. When applied during challenging circumstances, their faithfulness inevitably leads the team to happy outcomes.

Who Will You Listen To?

As the Decision-Maker, the kind of experience you have in life and within your team is a direct result of your attitudes and behaviors. Here is a story to illustrate.

Once upon a time, a wise and loving grandparent was teaching their grandchild about life. Referencing the battle between Ego and Reason, the grandparent said, *"A fight is going on inside of me, and it is a terrible fight. It is between two wolves. One wolf represents feelings like fear, anger, guilt, arrogance, and sin. The other wolf represents feelings like trust, gentleness, defenselessness, and open-mindedness."*

Pausing a moment, the grandparent added, *"The same fight is going on inside of you and inside all human beings."*

After thinking about it for a minute or two, the grandchild asked, *"Which wolf will win?"*

The grandparent leaned forward and whispered, *"The one you feed."*

Puppeteer & Puppet

Another beautiful way to think about and embrace "you" as the Decision-Maker is to relate the real you to a puppet show. In this example, the Decision-Maker is the puppeteer, the one "behind the curtain," inside your mind.

Your attitudes and behaviors are your puppets. They are selected by your Decision-Maker and seen and heard by others as you demonstrate them daily "on stage" (as you go through your life). You control these puppets, these attitudes and behaviors, because you are the puppeteer, the Decision-Maker.

When you face difficult situations, it's critical to remember this truth and take control of your mind. When you remember who you are, you can consciously direct your attitudes and behaviors in an accountable, responsible, Right-Minded way.

> **RIGHT-MINDED Accountability** is the **desire, willingness,** and **ability** to change my mind & behavior in order to effectively respond to difficult situations.
>
> **This means owning my part in the situation by asking:**
>
> *"How did I CREATE, PROMOTE, or ALLOW this difficult situation to happen?"*
>
> RightMindedTeamwork.com

By taking control of your mind, you strengthen your:

> ...*desire*, **willingness**, *and* **ability** *to change your attitude and behavior to find a healthier way to respond to your difficult situation.*

Taking control of your mind, which can happen instantly, leads you to a mature and practical way of thinking and questioning.

That means you:

> ...*accept and own your part in the difficult situation by asking yourself, "How did I **create**, **promote**, or **allow** this situation to occur with my attitudes and behaviors?"*

It is easier to change your attitude and behavior when you consciously recognize and own your part as the puppeteer. You know you have the power to mitigate and possibly eliminate the problematic situation.

You Are the King & Queen

Here is one more way of thinking and describing you, the Decision-Maker. Imagine yourself as the king or queen of your kingdom.

Now, also imagine a problematic situation that arises as two warring tribes vie for your royal attention.

These warring tribes are your inner thoughts. They are very real to you, just like your dreams at night seem real until you awaken. These inner thoughts come from years of living and being programmed to value various life principles.

One tribe, led by Ego-based thoughts, loudly argues their case to you. They have come asking for your support, presenting themselves either as victims of the situation or as victimizers who believe you should help them launch a counterattack. This group's motto is, *"It wasn't my fault! You need to fix it and protect me."*

The other tribe, led by Reason, is not really interested in a war. Instead, Reason quietly offers win-win options that will heal and resolve the situation. Reason's tribe's motto is, *"I am not a victim of the world I see. I am here to be truly helpful."*

As the king or queen, once you have heard both sides, it is up to you to choose how you will respond to this difficult situation. Will you start an Ego-fueled war? Or will you be Right-Minded and accountable?

The choice is always yours.

What Attitudes Are You Feeding?

So, which wolf are you feeding? Which puppets are you choosing? As king or queen, which tribe are you listening to? The costs and benefits are clear.

If you want to transform any difficult situation, the first step is to shift your perspective by applying Lesson 1: *I am not upset for the reason I think.*

You must then acknowledge your own role by asking, *"What am I doing that contributes to creating, promoting, or allowing this situation to persist?"*

Exploring the answers to these questions will help you feed the Right-Minded tribe inside you, leading you to the best solutions for all.

The RMT Myth

A Message from Reason

Dear Reader,

My name is Reason. We have not been officially introduced, but I've been your constant supporter for many, many years.

Though you may think of me as an "I," I am not really a separate entity. I live inside of you. I also live inside everyone else, too. For that reason, it is more accurate to say, "We are Reason," collectively.

The story you are about to read will help you understand what I mean by that.

Here is a little preview:

> *Once, there was only Reason. Everyone had everything they needed, and everyone was happy with what they had.*
>
> *But out of nowhere, a tiny, mad idea crept into our collective minds. For just an instant, we began to wonder,*
>
> *"Is there more to be gained than what we have achieved by working together as one unified team?"*
>
> *This moment was the **birth of separation**.*

> *Fortunately, most of us just kindly laughed off the silly question. But some listened. They began to think separate thoughts. Some had the thought that if they could work alone and take more for themselves, it would make them even happier.*
>
> *Instead of following Reason's advice, they chose to follow Ego (the obvious instigator of such a thought).*
>
> *Because of their choice to break from Reason, teamwork faltered. Choosing to focus only on themselves impacted everyone.*

As you will see in the coming pages, there is more to this story. But even before you read it, allow this excerpt to prepare you. Open your mind to see the true value, importance, and power of *choice* – your choices, and the choices of your teammates.

In every situation, every one of us makes the choice to follow either Reason or Ego. The hope, of course, for the sake of your team's success, is that you and your teammates will choose Reason. When you do, you will do no harm, and you will always work as one.

The most beautiful part is that no matter how far you or your teammates may have strayed, by *choosing* to work *with* Reason, you will inevitably find your way back to collaborative, productive teamwork – your pre-separation state.

When following Reason, it is easy for teammates to make Right-Minded choices. It is natural for them to act and behave as a single, unified team, ready to achieve team goals.

The 7 Mindful Training Lessons and other RMT methods will teach you how to get there. With these tools, you and your team will create and follow your own Right-Minded thought system. You will develop Right-Minded, effective work processes.

Reader, I want you to know that I, Reason, am available to you anytime and anywhere, forever. When you are ready to collaborate and work together as a cohesive team, I will be there, in your mind, prepared to show you the way. Together, we will make it happen.

Then, you and your team will easily live the RMT motto. You will **do no harm** and **work as one**.

Join me on the Right-Minded Teamwork journey, a mindful inward journey to the goals you want to achieve.

Let's start today.

Forever yours,
~ Reason

PS - Don't hesitate to call on me anytime. It only takes a mindful moment. I am always here for you.

The Myth

Once, before we lived in tribes, we all naturally worked together as one.

All our needs were met. There was no sense of want because there was no need. Peace, abundance, and collaboration were normal. Instead of "yours" and "mine," we shared with each other simply and effortlessly.

There was no leader, either, but there was a clear, guiding spirit that emanated from our collective cooperation. We named that shepherding spirit **Reason**. Reason continually and gently reminded us of our caring thoughts and feelings for one another.

With Reason's guidance, there was no fear. There was no doubt as to who and what we were. We were one, always there for one another. We easily worked together. We needed and wanted each other. We had everything we could ask for.

But out of nowhere, a tiny, mad idea crept into our collective minds. For just an instant, we began to wonder,

> *Is there more to be gained than what we have achieved by working together as one unified team?*

This moment was the **birth of separation**.

Fortunately, most of us just kindly laughed off the silly question. But some listened. They began to think separate thoughts. Some had the thought that if they could work alone and take more for themselves, it would make them even happier.

Then Reason stepped gently into our collective minds and asked,

But how could we have more than everything?

Reason went on to remind us that we had free will. If we wanted, we could follow that foolish little thought. If we did, it would be just like falling asleep and having a bad dream. Fortunately, Reason assured us that if anyone fell asleep, we would not abandon them. All of us would remain here together, as one, to help them wake up.

For most of us, Reason's gentle question and kind words made sense. We decided Reason's advice was right for us. That decision was our first **moment of Reason**. Shifting our focus back to our teamwork, we continued to work together as one.

But not everyone agreed.

One, named **"Ego,"** concluded that if they had more than anyone else, it would make them even more special than Reason - or so they thought.

Ego didn't realize that this idea of being different and special was yet another tiny, mad idea. In the world of Oneness, everyone is on the same team, working towards the same goals for the same reasons, contributing fully. There is no value in being an outlier, somehow different than the rest. What would that add to the team? Within the Unified Circle of Right-Minded Thinking, we are all one.

Still, Ego persisted, following the mad idea, and seeking their own way until they began to fall asleep, just as Reason had predicted. As Ego's eyes closed, Reason tenderly placed a folded note alongside Ego. On the outside, it read, *"Open when you are ready to wake up."* On the inside, Reason included practical ideas on how to move back into the Unified Circle of Right-Minded Thinking. Eventually, this vital information would help Ego return.

But let's continue with the story. Fast asleep, Ego didn't notice Reason's gesture or note. To the slumbering Ego, the plan was crystal clear: Get more by taking more from others—more of... everything.

So off Ego went, taking more and more. Even though there was enough for everyone, Ego continued to take extra. But soon, Ego ran into a problem: Where to store all the extra stuff so no one would take it back?

Ego decided to leave and find a place to hide the stuff, somewhere no one could see it or steal it.

Proud of having such an excellent plan, Ego struck up a conversation with some others on the way to taking more stuff to hide. Ego bragged about all the really good stuff already stored away and the excellent plan to acquire even more. Ego even claimed to have more than Reason, which of course, was not true. Ego's illusion - *delusion* - made Ego feel special and important.

Regrettably, Ego was able to convince a few others to join in. They wanted Ego's version of specialness, too. Each of them began taking more, just like Ego.

They called their new group a tribe. Reason, and all those still following Reason's attitudes and Right-Minded Thinking, called them the Separated Ones. For a little while, the separated tribe sort of worked… until one day, a tribe member took stuff from another tribe member.

Now there was conflict. Conflict was a new feeling; no one had experienced it before. Other new emotions, like anger, fear, revenge, grievance, and doubt began showing up in the tribe members' minds as well. Everyone agreed these new feelings were awful. They convinced themselves and each other that their only hope of getting rid of those dreadful feelings was to go out and take more stuff. They tried to cover their fear with *more* - which, in truth, never works.

Soon, the tribe member who lost stuff to the other member became incredibly angry and hostile. They couldn't stand it any longer. A new question crept in: How could they each protect their stuff?

One more tiny, mad, Ego-driven idea arose in their mind:

> *I know what I'll do! I'll leave this tribe and start my own tribe.*

From that moment on, more and more tribe members began to join and split off, then join and split again, over, and over. Eventually, their wrong-minded choices created the world we live in today: a world filled with adversaries where once there were only allies.

Today, we have thousands of tribes around the globe taking from one another in more physical and psychological ways than we can possibly count. We live in a complex world of duality and chaos. A world of yours and mine. A world where, far too often, people fight over and take each other's stuff.

Most of us who are stuck in wrong-minded thought systems do not even know we are stuck. Fortunately, as napping Egos, we are only asleep in a nightmarish and chaotic dream where every choice leads to greater dysfunction.

We are dreaming of separation, but in reality, we are still one. If we choose, we can still follow Reason. We can begin our journey back to Right-Minded Teamwork and the unified circle of Oneness. It's not too late to wake up.

Waking up means first gently accepting the fact that, as long as we view ourselves as our Egos, we are *out of our Right Minds*.

Once we accept this - our first **moment of Reason** - we will discover Reason's note, apply the sage advice, and gladly embrace Right-Minded attitudes and behaviors.

Moral of the Story

Wake up.

Shift your perspective.

Return to the Unified Circle of Right-Minded Thinking.

No matter what happens, and no matter how real it may feel or appear, Ego's world is a dream. As a team leader, teammate, or team facilitator, **your new purpose** is to partner with Reason to awaken your teammates from their negative, adversarial nightmare and show them how to choose Reason, too.

As you do, you will invite them to participate in creating your team's Right-Minded thought system. This set of team beliefs and behaviors will bring all teammates back into collaborative unity, allowing you to work together as one team.

Reason's Personal Note to You

Do you remember in the Right-Minded Teamwork Myth when, as Ego was falling asleep, Reason tenderly placed a folded note alongside Ego? On the outside, it read, *"Open when you are ready to wake up."* On the inside were practical ideas on how to move back into the Unified Circle of Right-Minded Thinking.

Now that you are ready to wake up and help your teammates wake up, too, it is time to read what Reason wrote. You unfold the note and read...

We are Reason

Before you listened to Ego and embraced the tiny, mad idea of separation, everyone stood inside the Unified Circle of Right-Minded Thinking. We were One. We were, collectively, Reason.

You know this to be true. Your own experience has taught you this. There have been times, even in your separated life, when all your needs were met. There was no sense of want because you had what you needed. That experience reflects your pre-separation state.

You have also felt, in the past, safe and secure in Reason's way of living and working with your brothers and sisters.

Remember those moments of Reason. Restore your mind to Reason, follow your intuition, shift your perspective, and your Right-Minded behaviors will tenderly flow through you to your teammates.

Of course, to simply say these words means nothing. You must live these words. Then, they will mean everything.

Choose to step inside the Right-Minded circle of unified teamwork and gently and firmly train your mind and heart to remember your pre-separation state. Say to yourself, "I can elect to change all thoughts of separation. Choosing anything but working together as one unified team is nothing but a dream."

This is the truth.

Within your team and within yourself, it must be said, then repeated many times. At first, it will be accepted as partially true with many reservations. Over time, it will be considered seriously, more and more, until it is finally accepted as truth.

Come back!

Stand confidently inside the circle. Draw your teammates back into living Right-Minded Teamwork behaviors. By drawing your teammates back, you strengthen Reason's way of living in this world for your brother, your sister, and yourself.

Now, follow these instructions. Apply the 5 Elements of Right-Minded Teamwork and the 9 Right Choices. Apply the 7 Mindfulness Lessons of Right-Minded Thinking. And begin your journey back to the place of Oneness from which you came.

~ Reason

This story, the Right-Minded Teamwork process, the Right-Minded Teamwork Attitudes & Behaviors, and the RMT Choice Model were inspired by *A Course in Miracles.*

7 Mindfulness Training Lessons

For Right-Minded Teamwork Thinking

1. I am not upset about this difficult team situation for the reason I think.

2. I accept and own my part in this situation.

3. It's impossible that my thoughts about this situation are neutral.

4. I forgive others and myself.

5. I will transform the effects of this difficult team situation.

6. I adjust my thinking and behavior.

7. I see every difficult team situation as a learning opportunity.

Applying the 7 Lessons

Let's take a closer look at the sentence from earlier that sums up the 7 Lessons:

I accept, forgive, and adjust my thinking and work behavior to effectively respond to difficult team situations.

More specifically, let's look at these three words: **accept**, **forgive**, and **adjust**. Those three words describe your mindful willingness to look within and choose how to respond to any and every situation you encounter. They guide you and show you how to look within.

These three concepts, along with four more, *are* the *7 Mindful Training Lessons*.

You must look within because that is where you will discover your **moment of Reason**. Your moment of Reason opens the door to finding Right-Minded answers, and true solutions that correct mistakes and resolve difficult team situations.

Looking within requires monitoring your thoughts, paying attention to the conversations you have with others, and being honest with yourself. Monitoring your thoughts and conversations *is* looking within.

Looking within and deciding to make mindful, Right-Minded choices, even in the midst of chaos, yields mature work behavior instead of Ego-driven, reactive conflict. This Right-Minded behavior increases the likelihood of transforming any difficulty into a safe learning experience.

To illustrate how all 7 Lessons are applied in your mind, we will use a situation you likely know very well: The Constantly Complaining Teammate (CCT).

A Constantly Complaining Teammate's various complaints may look or sound different day to day, but usually, a similar message underpins them all.

They consistently insist, *"My life can't get better until you change."*

They believe they are right. They think you and everyone else are wrong. For that reason, they are the perfect candidate for us to use as we explore the 7 Mindfulness Training Lessons.

Acceptance

The first two of the 7 Lessons can be summarized by the word **accept**.

Right-Minded Teammates do not blame others or try to shirk responsibility. They accept their role in all team functions, especially when difficult team situations arise and conflicts happen.

Right-Minded Teammates are committed to using their minds, not their emotions, to resolve conflict. They accept responsibility and are therefore willing to practice and learn these 7 Lessons. They know the Lessons will eventually bring them back to the Unified Circle of Right-Minded Thinking.

When a conflict arises, the first step in the 7 Lessons' mindfulness practice is to accept the difficult situation by going through two periods:

1. A period of **new awareness** (Lesson 1)

2. A period of **ownership** (Lesson 2)

These periods may last only a few minutes, but more often, especially when you first start using these Lessons, they might last longer. Also, they don't need to be painful, though they usually are at first.

Let's look at how the concept of acceptance plays out in the first two Lessons and with the Constantly Complaining Teammate.

7 Mindfulness Training Lessons

For Right-Minded Teamwork Thinking

1. I am not upset about this difficult team situation for the reason I think.

2. I accept and own my part in this situation.

3. It's impossible that my thoughts about this situation are neutral.

4. I forgive others and myself.

5. I will transform the effects of this difficult team situation.

6. I adjust my thinking and behavior.

7. I see every difficult team situation as a learning opportunity.

Lesson #1 – I Am Not Upset

I am not upset
about this difficult team situation
for the reason I think.

The word "upset" can mean many different things, such as anger, fear, anxiety, guilt, or shame. Whenever you are in a challenging situation, take a moment to carefully select the term that most accurately describes what you are experiencing and feeling.

It is essential to accurately identify the pain you are experiencing because it will help you see the connection between the current situation and something that happened in your past.

To give you an example, in the RMT book *Right-Minded Teamwork: 9 Right Choices for Building a Team That Works as One*, the sixth choice discusses focusing on the "critical few" as a way to address a team's "full-plate syndrome." First, though, teams must understand that underneath this surface syndrome is a root cause of collective fear, driven by Ego, that they will get in trouble if they do not do it all. If you also have that book, reread Choice #6 to help you apply this first Lesson.

Any time we experience pain in our interactions with others, we must learn to accept that our pain comes mostly from us, not them. Emotional pain is almost always rooted in the belief that whatever difficulty we are facing is somehow hurting us. For instance, a tough work situation might challenge your sense of self-worth. Or perhaps something has caused you to feel you are not receiving your just due.

No matter the difficulty, when an experience evokes past memories, we almost always react more strongly and less consciously because of the past association.

This *is why you are not upset for the reason you think.*

Once you are aware that *your* history and beliefs influence your experience, you will start to see that the challenge you are facing stems mainly from your own emotional reaction. When the present moment reminds you of when you were wronged or hurt in the past, your old memories of those times make the present situation seem far more painful.

That's not to say your teammates don't need to change. It only means you should not place responsibility on them for something that happened in *your* past.

When you notice you are upset (perhaps with a Constantly Complaining Teammate), stop whatever you are doing.

Compassionately say to yourself:

I am not angry at _____ for the reason I think.

I am not afraid of _____ for the reason I think.

I am not worried about _____ for the reason I think.

I am not depressed about _____ for the reason I think.

Taking this honest look within will help you identify unresolved memories. For example, you might have had a sibling or a schoolmate who constantly complained. Instead of being coached and corrected, they were rewarded and promoted, and you have always felt it was unfair. ***Listen carefully***: Though that happened many years ago, it is your belief in unfairness that is still upsetting you today. You must accept and own that you are emotionally reliving your own hurtful memories.

No matter what happened in the past, practicing mindfulness means that when difficult situations happen, you consciously choose to move back to your Right Mind in the present moment. This pivotal decision shifts any fixed perspectives, allowing you to move from attack to forgiveness.

Accepting your role and the influence of your past doesn't mean the CCT behavior you observe is acceptable. It merely means you are choosing not to let *their* behavior rule *your* mind or trigger your emotions. If you genuinely want to "live in a world that you rule instead of one that rules you," as I asked at the beginning of this book, the first step is taking control of your mind.

The first of the 7 Mindful Training Lessons, "I am not upset for the reason I think," creates an initial period of renewed awareness and acceptance. In other words, Lesson 1 triggers a **moment of Reason**. This is the place where your pain is lessened, and solutions are found.

Lesson 1 and your resulting moment of Reason are necessary precursors for the second Lesson, which will help you move back into your Right Mind.

Lesson #2 – I Accept

I accept and own my part in this situation.

When a difficult situation happens, you can either:

1. Fearfully believe Ego's guidance, and act like a victim or victimizer, or
2. Joyfully accept Reason's help and act in an accountable, Right-Minded way.

At all times, you are either mindful or mindless. You are either following your Right Mind, Reason, or your wrong mind, Ego.

In difficult team situations, the *Right-Minded Teamwork Choice Model* offers a tool for practicing mindfulness. Specifically, it asks you to go within by asking yourself, your Decision-Maker, the following question:

"What did I do to create, promote, or allow the CCT teammate to _____?"

Even though a Constantly Complaining Teammate is tough to work with, everyone on the team plays a part in the situation. Other teammates' behavior, including yours, is in some way enabling or triggering that teammate to continue complaining.

> **RIGHT-MINDED**
> **Accountability**
>
> is the **desire, willingness,** and **ability** to change my mind & behavior in order to effectively respond to difficult situations.
>
> **This means owning my part in the situation by asking:**
>
> *"How did I CREATE, PROMOTE, or ALLOW this difficult situation to happen?"*
>
> RightMindedTeamwork.com

In our example, here's how the Right-Minded Teammate's Decision-Maker might answer this compelling question. Look carefully for the concepts of creating, promoting, and allowing.

> *When I talk with [the CCT] while he's complaining, I communicate in a derisive, argumentative way. This makes him complain even more. My choices and way of interacting are part of what is **creating** this difficulty.*
>
> *I often complain about him behind his back. He may know I've done this, which probably frustrates him further, and that could easily make him complain even more. My own complaints are **promoting** this difficulty.*
>
> *When I see him coming my way in the hall, I quickly turn away to ensure we don't bump into one another just because I don't want to deal with his complaints or address the issue through confrontation. My avoidance behavior is **allowing** him to continue complaining.*

By asking yourself what you may be creating, promoting, or allowing, you will quickly learn to accept and own your part in any situation. Doing so is being honest with yourself. It is being mindful. This question strengthens your willingness to accept your **moment of Reason**, which will eventually lead to a Work Agreement with your complaining teammate.

Learning to accept your reactions and responsibility for your experience are essential steps in transforming your mind. They do not excuse your teammate's behavior. Rather, they are the foundation for seeing your teammates as classmates and allies. Accepting that you are not upset for the reason you think and owning your part in the difficult situation places you in the right mindset for doing no harm and working with your teammates as one.

Now that you have a sense of the importance of **acceptance** and how it is a crucial part of the first two Lessons, let's dive into the next three Lessons, which can be summarized with another word: **forgive**.

Forgiveness

The 7 Lessons will not work if you do not, or choose not to, **forgive** yourself and others.

Training your mind to forgive means you go through:

3. A period of **sorting out** your positive, negative, forgiving, and unforgiving thoughts (Lesson 3)

4. A period of **letting go** by forgiving yourself and others for negative or unforgiving thoughts and behaviors associated with this difficult situation (Lesson 4)

From there, you and your teammates can move into:

5. A period of **discovering new solutions** (Lesson 5)

These three periods can last for a while. As with acceptance, the process of forgiveness need not be painful, though it often is. However, as you apply these three forgiving Lessons more and more often, the stages will shorten and become less painful. This is one of the benefits of the process.

7 Mindfulness Training Lessons

For Right-Minded Teamwork Thinking

1. I am not upset about this difficult team situation for the reason I think.

2. I accept and own my part in this situation.

3. It's impossible that my thoughts about this situation are neutral.

4. I forgive others and myself.

5. I will transform the effects of this difficult team situation.

6. I adjust my thinking and behavior.

7. I see every difficult team situation as a learning opportunity.

Lesson #3 – No Neutral Thought

*It is impossible that my thoughts
about this difficult situation are neutral.*

Your thoughts are never neutral.

Thoughts always produce Right-Minded or wrong-minded emotions and behaviors. It happens whether you are awake or asleep, whether your thinking is mindful or mindless.

Remember, your thoughts can take you in only two directions. They can move you toward Right-Minded Thinking, including acceptance, forgiveness, and adjustment. Or they can just as quickly move you in the opposite direction toward rejection, attack, and defensiveness.

Let's revisit the difficult Constantly Complaining Teammate situation.

Whether this situation provokes Right-Minded Thinking or wrong-minded thinking for you, every person on your team experiences the effects of *your thoughts* about the CCT situation.

Why? Because your teammates can sense when you are having a bad and unforgiving day.

They can also sense when you're in a forgiving mood. You likely find people are drawn to you when you are in that state of mind. People can sense your openness. They know you won't blame them. They trust you and want your advice.

So, wherever your thoughts take you, admit it. Own it. Stop pretending you can hide your thoughts and feelings.

You can't. No one can.

But you can be honest about them.

No matter what you are feeling, you can communicate in a Right-Minded way that guarantees the kind of teammate relationships you want.

To create a Right-Minded relationship, you must first stop yourself from reacting negatively when you notice you are upset. In that **moment of Reason**, kindly say to yourself:

This thought about _____ (situation) is not a neutral thought.

That thought about _____ (person) is not a neutral thought.

I accept that my thoughts about _____ are not neutral because it is impossible for me to hide my thoughts.

As you look honestly at your negative, Ego-driven thoughts, remember they are causing you pain. They are also preventing you from finding reasonable solutions.

Stop and think carefully about this:

When you recognize that your past makes it impossible to have neutral thoughts... And you can identify those non-neutral, negative thoughts when they arise...

You are naturally motivated to move from wrong-minded thinking into positive, Right-Minded thoughts and attitudes, which are likely captured in your team Work Agreements.

When you make this shift, your teammates will sense you are ready to forgive and find solutions. You will find them far more open and receptive once you have shifted to Right-Minded Thinking.

Now that you have calmed yourself down by taking control of your mind, it's time to forgive yourself and others.

Lesson #4 – I Forgive

I forgive myself and others.

Anger. Fear. Anxiety. Guilt. Shame. Judgment.

All of these are similar feelings, and they are all part of being human.

However, they are never justified because angry and fearful thoughts and emotions like these are, at their core, blocks to accessing your Right Mind. They prevent you from finding the right answers to difficult situations.

Forgiving yourself and others for having these emotions will eventually make you feel safe. Doing so also means you are willing to accept your part in the situation because you know you will not be punished. Removing judgment allows you to discover the real root of the conflict. With this clarity, your team can resolve the situation.

Forgiving, or not judging, is the only way to create a Right-Minded team atmosphere. The fact that forgiveness, not judgment, is Right-Mindedness is illustrated by the below quote from *A Course in Miracles*.

> *He who would not forgive must judge, for he must justify his failure to forgive. But he who would forgive himself [and others] will learn to welcome the truth exactly as it is.*

Forgiveness, combined with acceptance and adjustment, is the only effective, sane response to difficult team situations. It is also your only natural response to a difficult situation. Lesson 4 reminds you that attack, blame, and judgment are unnatural.

When you notice unforgiving thoughts toward others, such as the CCT, quietly say to yourself, *"I am not upset about his complaining for the reason I think. I own my part and forgive myself, at least this time, for resisting, defending, and not listening to his complaints."*

The more you forgive, the more you will see what Right-Minded Thinking, and specifically these 7 Lessons, can do for you.

Lesson #5 – I Transform

*I will transform the effects
of this difficult team situation.*

Being mindful of your thoughts and being willing to change them is the only way to transform how you see and interact with the Constantly Complaining Teammate.

This is because your thoughts determine what you experience on your team.

To transform what you see happening in your team, especially in difficult situations, you must consciously change course. You must recognize the direct effects of your "Ego attack thoughts" and be willing to give them up.

"Attack thoughts" are the opposite of forgiving thoughts. It doesn't matter whether your attack thoughts of irritation or frustration are mild or intense. Do not believe Ego's argument that mild irritation is somehow not as bad. It is still an attack thought you are projecting. The specifics of the situation don't matter, either. Every unforgiving attack thought inevitably moves you into wrong-minded thinking, seeing, and behaving.

As always, you have only two choices: Attack and stay in prison. Or accept, forgive, and adjust and create a wonderful, safe classroom.

The more mental attacks you do, the more trapped you become in your personal prison. Fortunately, as the Decision-Maker, King or Queen, and Puppeteer, you always have the power to choose the path you want. All you have to do is make a choice to shift your thinking, and you will create a different experience by opening yourself to a **moment of Reason**. In that moment, you will move from the battleground to the classroom.

Here's how to do it. When you notice yourself having Ego-minded attack thoughts, stop, and compassionately and firmly say to yourself:

I will transform the effects of _____ by remembering the power of choice is mine. I determine how I feel about this situation, not the other way around.

I will transform the effects of this difficult team situation by giving up these attack thoughts about _____.

Instead of seeing _____ (situation or person) as an attack, I will interpret their behaviors as a call for help – for my help.

Genuinely relinquishing negativity in this way can be incredibly freeing.

Now, you are committed and prepared to **do no harm** and **work as one** with your Constantly Complaining Teammate.

Once you have accomplished these first five Lessons on **acceptance** and **forgiveness**, you are ready for the final two Lessons of Right-Minded Thinking, which focus on **adjustment**.

Adjustment

Let's review where we are in applying the 7 Mindfulness Training Lessons with the Constantly Complaining Teammate.

By **accepting** Lessons 1 (I am not upset for the reason I think) and 2 (I own my part), you realized you only temporarily fell prey to wrong-minded thinking. Then, you were able to shift your perspective into a place of **forgiveness** with Lessons 3 (My thoughts cannot be neutral), 4 (I forgive myself and others), and 5 (I transform).

Now that you have transformed your perception, accepted the CCT, and forgiven yourself and all others involved, you are ready for the final two Lessons, which involve **adjusting** your thinking.

When you do, your efforts help transform the CCT relationship. You also help heal all the collateral damage that was created.

As you train your mind and adjust the way you think, you will go through:

6. A period where you **experience the benefits** of your new way of thinking (Lesson 6)

7. A period of Right-Minded Thinking **achievement** (Lesson 7)

Unlike the Acceptance and Forgiveness stages, which can be painful and take a while, the adjustment stage often occurs quite naturally. Here's how it works.

7 Mindfulness Training Lessons

For Right-Minded Teamwork Thinking

1. I am not upset about this difficult team situation for the reason I think.

2. I accept and own my part in this situation.

3. It's impossible that my thoughts about this situation are neutral.

4. I forgive others and myself.

5. I will transform the effects of this difficult team situation.

6. I adjust my thinking and behavior.

7. I see every difficult team situation as a learning opportunity.

Lesson #6 – I Adjust

I adjust my thinking and behavior.

Remember: If you always do what you have always done, you will always get what you have always gotten.

Read that sentence again. Let it soak in.

To create a positive working relationship with the CCT, you cannot continue exhibiting the same attitude and behavioral patterns. You cannot keep thinking and doing what you've always done. If you do, nothing changes. They will simply continue complaining.

You also cannot force them to change. So, the only way to change the pattern and the relationship is to change yourself. Specifically, you must change how you think about them. You must move from wrong-minded thinking to Right-Minded Thinking.

When you first start training your mind and adjusting your thinking, you will likely find yourself slipping back into old ways. You may even feel inner resistance as you try to shift your old thought patterns.

For this reason, it is okay (and even advisable) to start with small changes in your thoughts and behaviors.

Each time you listen to your positive intuition and apply the ideas you have learned, you will see a positive change between you and your teammates. This proof will inspire you to continue onward. As you begin to trust the process, it will become easier to adjust further.

Here's how a positive, intuitive conversation might sound inside your mind:

When I know I have to talk to [the CCT], I will be kind and compassionate toward him.

I'll remind myself I am in charge of what I think, do, and say. Only I decide what I think and do in response to whatever he's complaining about. I will remember my commitment to do no harm and work as one.

The next time he complains, the first thing I'll do is let go of my own mental resistance and just accept what is happening. Secondly, I'll actively listen to his ideas to see if I can find a legitimate solution. My goal is simply to bring him to his senses, not to his knees.

I will freely share my opinion, but I'll communicate it in an emotionally mature way, even if he is still actively complaining. In other words, just because he is listening to his Ego and practicing wrong-minded thinking doesn't mean I have to think or speak the same way.

When I act and behave as a Right-Minded Teammate, he will experience good, mindful teamwork behavior firsthand. He might even decide to change, too!

No matter what transpires, we will create a Work Agreement on how we will work together as Right-Minded Teammates.

Lesson #7 – I Learn

*I see every difficult team situation
as a Right-Minded Teamwork learning opportunity.*

You have witnessed the transformative power of the 7 Mindfulness Training Lessons firsthand and have reached the final period of achievement. You are now in control of your kingdom – your mind.

More and more often, you mindfully say to yourself:

> *I accept that I am not my mistakes. Mistakes are opportunities.*
>
> *I am determined to convert my mistakes and learn from them.*
>
> *I am kind and compassionate toward others, as I ask them to be toward me. I always think and behave in a "we-centered" way.*
>
> *I'm not a victim of the world I see. I determine how I feel about a situation or change, not the other way around.*
>
> *I am committed to do no harm and to work as one.*
>
> *I believe that none of us is as smart as all of us.*
>
> *I am confident [the CCT] and I can and will create a Work Agreement that will work for both of us.*

Enjoy this period of achievement. You deserve it.

Also, remember: There will always be another difficult team situation that will upset you. It may be the same complaining teammate or a completely new challenge.

Fortunately, these subsequent situations will have less impact on you. They will become less and less painful. Why? Because you are in control of your mind. You are the King and Queen of *your* mind. You know you are *your* Puppeteer.

When a new difficult situation arises, you no longer react. You go straight back to the very first Lesson of Right-Minded Thinking. You say:

I am not upset about this difficult team situation for the reason I think.

I am determined to see _____ [name of person] differently.

I am determined to see this situation differently.

I am determined to see _____ [their attribute, i.e., complaining] differently.

You remember Reason's guidance from the note left for you, the one written to help you awake from Ego's dream of separation.

There, Reason said:

> *Come back!*
>
> *Stand confidently inside the Unified Circle of Right-Minded Thinking. Draw your teammates back into living Right-Minded Teamwork behaviors. By drawing your teammates back, you strengthen Reason's way of living in this world for your brother, your sister, and yourself.*
>
> *Follow these instructions. Apply the 5 Elements of Right-Minded Teamwork and the 9 Right Choices. Apply the 7 **Mindfulness Lessons of Right-Minded Thinking**. And begin your journey back to the place of Oneness from which you came.*
>
> *~ Reason*

You apply the 7 Lessons once more, trusting in their proven power. As you enter your classroom, you smile, knowing that every time you call on Reason by choosing Right-Minded Thinking, you move yourself and your team towards **doing no harm** and **working as one**.

The Choice Is Always Yours

By now, this statement should be crystal clear and easy to accept:

The only freedom you truly have is your freedom to choose.

To make the most of your freedom, you must consistently apply Reason's 7 Mindfulness Training Lessons, no matter what situation you face.

To do that, you must first train your mind.

When you have sufficiently trained your mind, you also join others who hold these mindful truths to be self-evident. You know that all minds are created equal, and whosoever believes in the Oneness of equal minds will have everlasting freedom to choose Right-Minded Teamwork.

What Does It Mean to "Train Your Mind?"

Training your mind simply means practicing Right-Minded Thinking as often as possible by consistently applying the 7 Lessons in difficult team situations.

When your mind is well-trained, and a difficult team situation happens, you immediately and silently speak the Lessons to yourself and listen for Reason's guidance.

By actively asking questions, and then stepping back to listen for the answers, you will learn to hear and trust Reason's voice implicitly. The Lessons are catalysts that carry you deeper into your Right Mind, where you hear the best answers to the questions you ask.

How do you know you are listening to the voice of Reason?

First, you know you've heard Reason when you're at peace.

Secondly, the answer you have received heals the difficulty while doing no harm to anyone.

If your solution meets both tests, rest assured you have listened to Reason and will soon be working as one.

Once you have those answers, you will always know how to behave and respond. You forgive your teammates' errors and mistakes by recognizing them, accepting them, transforming your perspective about them, and immediately moving toward finding solutions.

Summarizing the CCT Transformation

Here's another way to know you have **successfully trained your mind** and shifted your perspective to find solutions using the 7 Mindful Training Lessons.

Ask yourself: What do you *"see"* when you interact with a Constantly Complaining Teammate?

If what you see in your mind's eye is a big angry dog, ready to attack you and others, you are seeing them from your Ego's perspective. If your teammate appears that way to you, you believe they are to be feared and avoided. Think about that for a moment. If the errors and mistakes you see in them look vicious, you are holding an *untrained* and *unforgiving* perspective in your wrong mind.

But when you *desire* to be mindful of your thoughts and train your mind, your beliefs and perspectives will most certainly change with Reason's guidance. Now, instead of seeing your CCT as a vicious dog ready to attack, the *shift* into your Right Mind – your new perception – now shows you a cute, albeit angry, little puppy. It is now *impossible* to fear your teammates, and there is certainly no valid reason to avoid them.

They Are Asking for Help

When you successfully train your mind and make this shift, you experience a **moment of Reason**, opening you to hear Reason's positive and healing solutions.

With your new and healed perspective, you don't see their complaints as attacks. You reinterpret their complaints as mistakes that need correction, not punishment. You accept their complaints as *their call for help,* not justification for an attack.

Note that nothing on the outside has changed about your complaining teammate. Only the way you choose to perceive them has changed. Now that you are able to see them and their mistakes differently, you know there is nothing to fear, resist, or avoid. You finally see your CCT for who they really are.

Instead of reacting negatively, you say to yourself:

I will listen to their complaints. I'll ask clarifying questions to be sure I fully understand.

I will do my best to forgive this person for their constantly complaining behavior because I honestly think they care about doing a good job, even if they communicate poorly.

I will be kind, compassionate, non-judgmental, and civil in the way I respond. I will not get defensive. I will do no harm. I'll ask how we should resolve the situation.

I will say silently to myself, "You are not a violent, angry dog ready to attack me. You're a scared little puppy who is calling out to me and others for help. I was wrong to see you as an angry dog. You deserve our compassion and support.

No matter what, we will create a Work Agreement as to how we will collaboratively work together going forward.

The more you apply Reason's Lessons and train your mind, the more all the CCTs in your life will come to look less and less like big angry dogs and more and more like cute little puppies that want to be helped, held, and petted. They truly deserve no less than your Right-Minded, caring, and loving response.

> *Rather than a person to be feared, avoided, harmed, or dismissed, your teammate is a worthy sister or brother who wants to be heard, included, and helped – by you and your teammates.*

It is indeed a happy discovery to learn you have the power to change your mind!

Your New, Mindful Journey Begins

The more often you apply the 7 Mindfulness Training Lessons, the more you'll realize that Right-Minded Thinking is far more than just a simple set of steps or a conflict resolution tool.

Right-Minded Thinking is a transformational journey.

> *It is a journey without distance to the best version of yourself.*

It is also one of the most profitable journeys you will ever make. Only you can make this journey, but you're not the only one who benefits. Your teammates and customers benefit, too.

On this journey, you are never alone. You have mighty companions, including Reason, who guides you, and your fellow Right-Minded Teammates, who support you.

There are useful tools in Reason's classroom, including these 7 Lessons, the Right Choice Model, and many other RMT tools and concepts. All of these will help you achieve and sustain Right-Minded Thinking.

Also inside the classroom are your Right-Minded Teammates, who are calling you to join them. They invite you to enter and make yourself at home in the forgiving Unified Circle of Right-Minded Thinking.

Will you join them and embrace your Right-Minded journey?

Only you can choose. Choose well.

The End

Thanks for reading our Right-Minded Teamwork book *7 Mindful Training Lessons: Improve Teammates' Ability to Work as One with Right-Minded Thinking.* If you enjoyed it, wouldn't you please take a moment to leave a review at your favorite retailer or RightMindedTeamwork.com?

Also, in a few pages, you will find something beneficial: *a Glossary of Right-Minded Teamwork Terms and Resources.*

And finally, on behalf of Reason and all the Right-Minded Teammate Decision-Makers, we extend our best wishes to you and your teammates as they create another *Right-Minded Team that Works Together as One.*

About the Author

The idea of "developing people and teams that work" began as a company statement for organizational consulting firm Lord & Hogan LLC, founded in 1990. Leveraging his personable but results-oriented consulting style, founder **Dan Hogan** devoted his career to transforming dysfunctional work relationships into positive, supportive bonds.

But over the course of his 40-year career, something shifted.

Through his work as an organizational development coach, performance consultant, and Certified Master Facilitator, the mission of Lord & Hogan also became Dan's own.

Better Work Relationships = Stronger, More Productive Teams

As a consultant and facilitator, Dan advocated for the individuals and managed teams he served. He emphasized the equal importance of strong team member relationships and solid business systems and processes to overall business success. His efforts spoke for themselves as his clients began to notice results.

With Dan's guidance, teams were more productive almost overnight. There were fewer day-to-day interpersonal issues. Project management efforts were finally back on track. Teams were achieving their goals.

After being stuck for so long, these teams were moving forward... smoothly. As one client said, "Dan has the unique ability to hear the confusion and bring clarity. He has helped me, our team, and our organization to move to the next level."

The Right-Minded Teamwork Model: A Legacy

Not only did Dan's efforts deliver consistent, powerful results (gaining him many long-term clients over the years) at a higher level, but his work also positively impacted the practice of behavioral change management.

Over the course of his career, Dan refined his ideas along with the help of his clients and the teams he served. Eventually, he created his own proprietary tools, processes, and strategies. Of all his models and creations, Dan's most significant accomplishment has been the development of his Right-Minded Teamwork model, which perfectly assembles all his tools and processes into a single, streamlined approach.

At its core, Right-Minded Teamwork (RMT) is a continuous improvement loop for small and large groups; it has been proven to work with teams of all sizes. No matter what team challenges or interpersonal issues are happening, RMT has the power to correct them.

By first bringing the team together under a unified set of goals, and then providing tools for teams to explore, understand, and work through their underlying concerns, Right-Minded Teamwork provides teams with the opportunity to address unproductive behaviors in a safe, non-condemning way. Focusing on acceptance, forgiveness, and self-adjustment among teammates, Right-Minded Teamwork directly addresses and resolves the root cause of even the most difficult teamwork situations.

After directly serving over 500 teams in seven countries and creating lasting tools and resources that will go on to support countless additional teams, leaders, and facilitators on every continent, Dan Hogan has left a legacy to be proud of. No longer an active facilitator, Dan has transformed his ideas and contributions into powerful, effective, team-building tools available online, providing team facilitators and team leaders around the globe access to Right-Minded Teamwork.

Books by Dan Hogan

Reason, Ego & the Right-Minded Teamwork Myth: *The Philosophy and Process for Creating a Right-Minded Team That Works Together as One*

This book explores two foundational concepts: the Right-Minded Teamwork Myth, a short tale that presents RMT's underlying teamwork philosophy, and the Right-Minded Teamwork team-building process, a step-by-step approach to implementing RMT in any team.

Right-Minded Teamwork in Any Team: *The Ultimate Team-Building Method to Create a Team That Works as One*

Right-Minded Teamwork is built on a framework of 5 Elements, explored in this book. These two goals and three methods are implemented into your team through three team-building workshops conducted over a six-to-12-month period. Once your team completes their third workshop, you move into a 90-day, continuous improvement operating plan that allows your team to achieve their goals, do no harm and work together as one.

How to Facilitate Team Work Agreements: *A Practical, 10-Step Process for Building a Right-Minded Team That Works as One*

Team Work Agreements are collective pledges made by your team to transform non-productive or dysfunctional actions into positive and constructive work behavior. Though this book is written primarily for team facilitators, team leaders, and teammates may also follow these steps to create powerful, effective Work Agreements to solve and prevent interpersonal and process problems.

How to Apply the Right Choice Model: *Create a Right-Minded Team That Works as One*

The concept of Right Choice states every person has free will. Free will means you are 100% responsible for how you respond to every situation, circumstance, and event. When difficult team problems occur, you either act as an ally or an adversary. When you choose to be an ally, you demonstrate positive, accountable behavior. When you are an adversary, you behave as either a victim or a victimizer. This book and model will guide you through creating a team of productive, supportive, Right-Minded teammate allies.

7 Mindfulness Training Lessons*: Improve Teammates' Ability to Work as One with Right-Minded Thinking*

If you want your team to work together as one, you want them to think as one, too. These 7 Mindfulness Training Lessons will help you achieve a positive team mindset by guiding teammates to raise their awareness of thoughts, choices, and behaviors. Teammates may also use these lessons to create the team's Right-Minded thought system. The 7 Lessons can be summed up in one sentence, emphasizing three words: Right-Minded Teammates **accept**, **forgive**, and **adjust** their thinking and work behavior. When teammates follow these lessons, they **do no harm** while **working together as one.**

Right-Minded Teamwork*: 9 Right Choices for Building a Team That Works as One*

This quick read is an excellent Right-Minded Teamwork primer and a terrific way to introduce RMT to teammates. These nine teamwork choices are universal, self-evident, and self-validating. You want them in your team. In this book, each of the 9 Right Choices is defined, and exercises are provided for applying each choice.

Design a Right-Minded, Team-Building Workshop:
12 Steps to Create a Team That Works as One

This book includes complete instructions on how to design a practical, real-world, team-building workshop that teammates actually want to attend. Unlike many team activities labeled "team building" that are really more "team bonding," true team-building workshops are intentionally designed to solve a team's real-world problems. Written primarily for team facilitators, team leaders, and teammates may also follow these 12 steps to design an effective, transformative team workshop.

Achieve Your Organization's Strategic Plan*: Create a Right-Minded Team Management System to Ensure All Teams Work as One*

When a single team within an organization works together as one, they are effective and productive. When an enterprise works with the same level of synergy, it is exponentially more powerful. A Team Management System like the Right-Minded Teamwork TMS model taught in this book lays the groundwork for your organization to get every team on the same page. By following RMT's four-part rollout plan, you can create and deploy your own Team Management System, align teammate attitudes, and work behavior with company values, and bring your entire organization together to work as one and achieve your strategic plan.

Resources

To download RMT models and processes to give teammates, go to RightMindedTeamwork.com, and search for this book's companion *Reusable Resources & Templates*.

Glossary of Right-Minded Teamwork Terms & Resources

100% Customer Satisfaction

Creating 100% customer satisfaction is a primary goal of Right-Minded Teamwork. Your team is responsible for providing quality products and services to customers; for your team and enterprise to succeed, your customers deserve to be 100% satisfied.

With a strong customer satisfaction plan, as described in *Right-Minded Teamwork in Any Team*, your teammates will strive to achieve customer satisfaction while consistently achieving other business goals.

7 Mindfulness Training Lessons

Achieving Right-Minded Teamwork involves adopting an attitude of mindfulness. The *7 Mindfulness Training Lessons* teach you to think in a Right-Minded way, ensuring you **do no harm** as you **work as one** with your teammates.

These powerful lessons are summed up in one sentence, with emphasis on three words:

*Right-Minded Teammates **accept**, **forgive**, and **adjust** their thinking and work behavior.*

In every circumstance, especially during difficult team situations, Right-Minded Teammates practice mindfulness to move them from defensiveness and blame into a Right-Minded, allied way of thinking and behaving.

Inspired by *A Course in Miracles* and our Right Choice Model, the *7 Mindfulness Training Lessons* is a teaching tool designed to help those willing to apply them to ensure they return to the Unified Circle of Right-Minded Thinking.

Go to RightMindedTeamwork.com or visit your favorite book retailer to pick up your copy of ***7 Mindfulness Training Lessons***: *Improve Teammates' Ability to Work as One with Right-Minded Thinking.*

10 Characteristics of Right-Minded Teammates

Right-Minded Teammates have many different surface traits and personalities. They are not all alike. They have numerous backgrounds, vastly different experiences, and a wide range of skills.

Nevertheless, it is understood that the Right-Minded Teammate, in their own particular behavioral style, happily live these characteristics because they align the teammate's authentic *self* with their team's version of the RMT motto: *do no harm, work as one,* and *none of us is as smart as all of us.*

You will find a complete description of these characteristics in RMT's book: ***Right-Minded Teamwork in Any Team:*** *The Ultimate Team Building Method to Create a Team That Works as One.*

1. Trust	2. Honesty	3. Tolerance
4. Gentleness	5. Joy	6. Defenselessness
7. Generosity	8. Patience	9. Open-Mindedness
	10. Faithfulness	

12 Steps Workshop Design Process

Design a Right-Minded, Team-Building Workshop:*12 Steps to Create a Team That Works as One.* This book will teach you how to design a practical, real-world team-building workshop.

The 12 steps are grouped into three phases: Contract, Commence, and Carry on. Written primarily for team facilitators, team leaders, and teammates can easily follow the steps to design a successful team-building workshop. Because this method engages teammates in designing the agenda, it virtually guarantees that teammates *cannot wait* to attend the workshop. They *know* that they will get real work done in a safe, "no harm" environment when they meet.

A Course in Miracles

Oneness. Forgiveness is the key to happiness, inner peace, undifferentiated unity, and ultimately – *Oneness*. "A Course in Miracles (ACIM) is a unique spiritual self-study program designed to awaken us to the truth of our *Oneness* with God and Love," as posted on ACIM.org and ACIM.org/ACIM/en. See the Foundation for A Course in Miracles at FACIM.org, where Ken Wapnick, the founder, created this beautiful definition.

> *A Course in Miracles is a psychological approach to spirituality where forgiveness is the central theme, and inner peace is the result.*

ACIM and other moral and spiritual philosophies that advocate and help people everywhere **work together as One** has inspired Right-Minded Teamwork. We used Ken's definition as a guide to create the Right-Minded Teamwork definition.

> *Right-Minded Teamwork is a business-oriented, psychological approach to team building where acceptance, forgiveness, and adjustments are teammate characteristics, and 100% customer satisfaction is the team's result.*

All Right-Minded Teamwork methods, processes, and tools seamlessly work together to help you create and sustain a *Team That Works Together as* **One**.

Accept, Forgive, Adjust

These three terms are at the core of Right-Minded Teammate Attitudes & Behaviors. These verbs are also central to the 7 Mindfulness Training Lessons, which are summed up in the sentence, *Right-Minded Teammates* **accept***,* **forgive***, and* **adjust** *their thinking and work behavior.*

Furthermore, these three concepts are included in the definition of Right-Minded Teamwork:

> *Right-Minded Teamwork is a business-oriented, psychological approach to team building where* **acceptance**, **forgiveness**, *and* **adjustment** *are teammate characteristics, and 100% customer satisfaction is the team's result.*

Lastly, these terms are also incorporated as three of the five steps in the *Right Choice Model*, which describes accountable and responsible Right-Minded Teamwork behavior.

Ally or Adversary Teammate

Right-Minded Teamwork asserts that as teammates, you either work together as allies or pull apart, viewing each other as adversaries.

Allies work towards achieving team goals. Adversaries work towards individual elevation, which separates and divides the team.

To determine whether you are in an ally or adversary mindset, ask yourself, *Do I want to be right, or do I want our team to be successful?* Allies want to be part of a successful team. Adversaries want to be right, no matter the cost.

As an adversary, Ego persuades you to compete with your teammates. As an ally, Reason says the opposite. Reason gently reminds you that separateness prevents true success. There cannot be Oneness or collaboration where there is competition.

As the Decision-Maker, you choose to follow either Reason or Ego. You either collaborate or compete. You are an ally or adversary. There is no middle ground.

If you choose to follow Reason and become an ally, you embrace and live your team's Work Agreements. If you decide to follow Ego, you become an adversary, creating a battleground inside yourself and your team.

To transform competitive adversaries into collaborative allies, start by following the *Right Choice Model*, creating team *Work Agreements*, and applying the *7 Mindfulness Training Lessons*.

Avoidance Behavior

Even though the term "avoidance behavior" is not often mentioned in the Right-Minded Teamwork model or books, avoidance behavior is easy to detect in teammates and RMT processes. If you notice it occurring, from an RMT perspective, you can consider it wrong-minded, adversarial behavior.

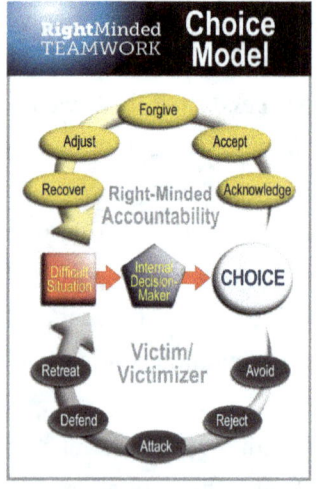

Identifying avoidance behaviors and attitudes and understanding the harm they cause is the first step in moving from a wrong-minded place into Right-Mindedness. The 7 Mindfulness Training Lessons and the Right Choice Model are excellent tools for teaching yourself and your team how to act and behave in a Right-Minded, accountable way.

For example, if you look carefully at the *Right Choice Model's* lower loop, you will notice that the victim or victimizer first avoids the situation when a difficult situation occurs.

When Right-Minded Teammates ask themselves the *Right Choice Model* question, *How did I **create**, **promote**, or **allow** this difficult situation to happen?* they often realize they have unconsciously demonstrated avoidance behavior. Then, noticing their mistake, they simply choose to **accept**, **forgive**, and **adjust** their approach and return to living in accordance with their team *Work Agreements*.

Battleground:
Where People Are Punished for Mistakes

The battleground represents wrong-minded thinking. It is a mental attitude or thought system that defends and encourages adversarial behaviors such as blame and attack.

Think of the battleground as a psychological symbol for those moments when you realize you are listening to Ego, not Reason (like when you notice avoidance behavior). You recognize that you are having an Ego attack for whatever reason and have made a wrong-minded choice. When you are in the battleground, you "punish" others for their mistakes, either by victimizing others or becoming a victim yourself.

On the other hand, when you are in your Right Mind, you see your team as a lovely and safe classroom, the opposite of the battleground. You do not punish others. You choose, instead, to rise above the conflict.

The purpose of recognizing the battlegrounds in your mind is to own the pain that you are causing yourself which helps you recognize that you consciously want to leave it, overlook it, rise above it, and to transport your mind into the classroom where you return to the forgiving Unified Circle of Right-Minded Thinking with your teammates.

Right-Minded Teammates working in safe and supportive classrooms do not fight, blame, or punish. Instead, they choose Oneness over separateness. They are committed to the team's success and achieving team goals.

To overcome a battleground in yourself or your team, go to RightMindedTeamwork.com, or visit your favorite book retailer to pick up your copy of *How to Apply the Right Choice Model: Create a Right-Minded Team That Works as One*. Inside, you will find a list of battleground attitudes and behaviors as well as the costs and benefits of classroom versus battleground thinking and behaving.

Certified Master Facilitator (CMF)

The Certified Master Facilitator (CMF) credential is a mark of excellence for facilitators. It is the highest available certification for facilitators. To learn more or to find a certified facilitator worldwide, visit the International Institute for Facilitation at INIFAC.org.

Classroom: Where People Learn from Mistakes

Like the battleground, the classroom is a symbol. But unlike the battlefield, where people punish or are punished, the classroom is where you learn and find inspiration.

At some point in your past, you have experienced the joy and wonder of learning. Right-Minded Teamwork invites you to view your team as a safe place to experience this wonder and joy as you learn new teamwork skills and collaborate to achieve team goals.

When you are experiencing fear in any form or realize you are having an Ego attack, you are in the battleground. To return to the classroom, say to yourself, *There is nothing to fear. In my mind, I choose to rise above this silly battleground and head to my Right-Minded classroom. There, we are committed to do no harm and work as one. There, we will find solutions.*

By recognizing the fear behind your Ego attack and reminding yourself to return to the classroom, you experience a **moment of Reason**. You also strengthen your Right-Minded thought system and restore yourself to Right-Minded Thinking.

In the RMT book *How to Apply the Right Choice Model: Create a Right-Minded Team That Works as One,* you will find a list of 30 Right-Minded and wrong-minded attitudes and behaviors, plus the associated costs and benefits to your team.

Communication Work Agreement

What you think – *your thought system* – drives your communication in one of two ways. You either communicate as a collaborative ally or as a competitive, dysfunctional, and emotionally immature adversary.

Teams that work as one and achieve their goals regularly seek out opportunities to improve communication. They take positive action by creating and living a Communication Work Agreement that describes their team's agreed-upon communication style.

Right-Minded communication is a core concept in the book ***Right-Minded Teamwork**: 9 Right Choices for Building a Team That Works as One,* available at RightMindedTeamwork.com or your favorite book retailer.

To create your team's Communication Work Agreement, follow the suggestions in the book ***How to Facilitate Teamwork Agreements**: A Practical, 10-Step Process for Building a Right-Minded Team That Works as One.*

In there, you will find two real examples of which one is a team Communication Work Agreement.

Create, Promote, Allow

These three concepts form the foundation of the *Right Choice Model's* essential question:

*How have I **created**, **promoted**, or **allowed** this situation to occur?*

Asking and honestly answering this question ensures teammates are "owning their part" in a difficult situation.

These three concepts are also integrated into *7 **Mindful Training Lessons**: Improve Teammates' Ability to Work as One with Right-Minded Thinking.*

High-performing Right-Minded Teammates always ask themselves this question because it leads them to solutions. It is a clear demonstration of the RMT motto, "**Do no harm. Work as one.**"

Critical Few:
Complete Important Tasks First

When a team is stuck in the "full-plate syndrome," identifying and completing the critical few - those tasks that have the largest and most direct impact on the team's success - is key to moving forward.

At the root of the full-plate syndrome is the **team's collective fear**, driven by Ego, which declares you will get in trouble if you do not do it all... even though the truth is you can never do it all.

People who listen to Ego believe they do not have a choice. Rather than realistically prioritizing their workload, they punish themselves for failing to meet the unreasonable goal of completing everything. They drain their energy, lose their focus, and make mistakes. They become powerless, cynical, and burned out.

But Reason reminds us that we always have this choice:

> *We can either win by doing the critical few tasks, or we can lose by attempting to do everything.*

Spend more time doing the right things right and let go of low-value tasks. Holding on to lower-value tasks is **not security**. It is **incarceration**.

The "critical few" concept is discussed in the book ***Right-Minded Teamwork***: *9 Right Choices for Building a Team That Works as One*.

See **Recognition: Make It Easy to Keep Going** for a related concept.

Decision-Maker: The Real You

Ken Wapnick, Ph.D., created the term "Decision-Maker" to define the "real you" in *A Course in Miracles*. For more on his work, visit FACIM.org.

Within Right-Minded Teamwork, the *Right Choice Model* uses the term "Decision-Maker" to describe the part of you that chooses to listen to and follow either the wrong-minded ways of Ego or the Right-Minded ways of Reason.

Your Decision-Maker is 100% responsible for who you choose to follow, what you choose to think, and how you choose to behave.

Right-Mindedness is achieved when you listen to and follow Reason. Listening means calming your Ego mind, trusting your intuition, and allowing space for a **moment of Reason** to arise.

When Right-Mindedness becomes an integral part of a team, the team consistently works together as one, doing no harm, within the forgiving Unified Circle of Right-Minded Thinking. When teammates do that, they are demonstrating and extending Right-Minded Teamwork to everyone.

To learn more about Reason, Ego, and the Decision-Maker, pick up the book *Reason, Ego, & the Right-Minded Teamwork Myth: The Philosophy & Process for Creating a Right-Minded Team That Works Together as One.*

Decision-Maker: Trust Your Intuition

If thinking about Reason and Ego is new to you, it can be helpful to think of Reason as your positive intuition and Ego as your negative, arrogant, and sometimes vindictive intuition.

At different times throughout our lives, we all have listened to and followed each of these teachers.

Stop and remember when you had a hunch or a feeling as to what you should do or say in a particular situation. Did you ignore your intuition? Let's say you did not follow your instinct, and it turned out to be a mistake. What did you say to yourself and others?

> *I wish I had trusted my intuition!*

As this memory illustrates, **you already know how to listen and be mindful** of your intuition. It is your natural, pre-separation state of mind [See **Oneness vs. Separateness**].

You just need to do it regularly.

Decision-Making Work Agreement

Every team needs a Decision-Making Work Agreement that clearly defines how decisions are made and who makes them. Creating a general agreement and putting it into your team's Operating System's Business Plan as a team Work Agreement makes good business sense.

If you do not currently have a Decision-Making team agreement or you have not updated it recently, I highly recommend you do that as soon as it is practical.

Incidentally, Decision-Making is #18 in the *Team Performance Factor Assessment* that you will use every 90 days to keep your team focused and on track. See **Team Operating System**.

In the book, ***How to Facilitate Team Work Agreements****: A Practical, 10-Step Process for Building a Right-Minded Team That Works as One,* you will find two real agreement examples. The first one is a behavioral team Communication Work Agreement, and the other is a Decision-Making Work Agreement. Check it out and use it as a model for your team's Decision-Making Work Agreement.

Desire & Willingness: Preconditions for Accountability

Even though the terms "desire" and "willingness" are not often mentioned in Right-Minded Teamwork materials (except within the *Right Choice Model*), Right-Mindedness and accountability are virtually synonymous.

The concepts of desire and willingness permeate all RMT methods and processes simply because it is impossible to think in a Right-Minded way, behave with Right-Minded Accountability, and achieve Right-Minded Teamwork without a heartfelt desire and genuine willingness to do so.

The Right Choice Model found in the book ***How to Apply the Right Choice Model***: *Create a Right-Minded Team That Works as One* teaches that *Right-Minded accountability is the desire and willingness to change my mind and behavior in order to effectively respond to difficult team situations.*

If you share the Right Choice Model with your team and distribute the Right Choice cards to teammates, you will see the definition of "desire and willingness" on the cards.

Do No Harm. Work as One.

The Right-Minded philosophy is founded on two universal truths:

Do No Harm.
Work As One.

None of us is as smart as all of us.
Right-Minded Teammates know that working collaboratively together, in a Right-Minded manner, is the only way to create the kind of teamwork that achieves and sustains 100% customer satisfaction. Said differently, these teammates genuinely want and need their fellow teammates.

Do no harm and work as one.
As a Right-Minded Teammate, you can be firm, direct, gentle, and compassionate, all at the same time. You do not blame yourself or others for mistakes. You and your teammates are allies, not adversaries, working together towards your shared goals.

Ego & Ego Attack

Ego is the negative, wrong-minded teacher who continually tells you how difficult the world is and how you must constantly fight to survive.

Reason is the opposite of Ego. Reason teaches you to *do unto others as you would have them do unto you.*

Ego believes everyone is out to get you and directs you to *do unto others before they do unto you.* Ego is also the creator of the tiny, mad idea of separation presented in the *Right-Minded Teamwork Myth*.

An Ego attack is a flash of negative, out-of-control emotion. It happens when you believe the awful feeling you are experiencing has been caused by something someone else said or did to you. Without thinking, you become behaviorally triggered; your body language, tone of voice, and the words you say become mean-spirited. An Ego attack is the opposite of a **moment of Reason**.

As soon as you realize you are experiencing an Ego attack, you must train your mind to say, *I am angry. I have lost control. I'm not upset for the reason I think. I am out of my Right Mind. I need a moment of Reason to gain control of my attitude. I must return to the classroom so I can find a Right-Minded way of replying that allows us to do no harm and work as one.*

Interlocking Accountability

Interlocking accountability is a crucial RMT concept that is primarily used in *How to Facilitate Team Work Agreements: a Practical, 10-Step Process for Building a Right-Minded Team That Works as One.*

When your team creates Work Agreements, it is highly recommended that one of your agreements includes an interlocking accountability statement so that teammates agree, ahead of time, how to compassionately confront a teammate who continues to break your Work Agreements.

Interlocking accountability means many things, including:

- Giving positive reinforcement when someone continues to do a great job of living the Work Agreements.
- Confronting someone in a supportive and safe but firm way if they continue to break the spirit or letter of the team's Work Agreement.
- Being accountable to each other for achieving or accomplishing the desired outcome of the Work Agreements.
- Recovering and learning from mistakes rather than denying or punishing those who make mistakes. This strengthens team spirit and trust.
- Creating and sustaining teammate trust because teammates who believe everyone will live their part of the Work Agreement will create Right-Minded Teamwork.

Moment of Reason

When you are facing a challenge such as an Ego attack, and you experience a positive and perhaps surprising moment of revelation, clarity, or sanity, you have achieved a moment of Reason.

These moments occur when you genuinely try to move from the battleground into the classroom. When Reason's teaching breaks through, you move from wrong-mindedness into Right-Mindedness.

Moments of Reason are magnificent. They are a cornerstone of your Right-Minded thought system. When they happen, you feel confident and at peace. You know what you should do, what to say, and to whom.

In moments of Reason, you know beyond a shadow of a doubt that you want and need your teammates. You easily return to the Unified Circle of Right-Minded Thinking, where teammates forgive one another, do no harm, and work as one.

Onboarding New Teammates

When a new leader or teammate joins your team, it is vitally important to properly onboard them within their first week on the job. In a single short meeting where everyone attends, the onboarding is easily and effectively accomplished.

Present all your RMT goals and Work Agreements along with why they were created. They ask you clarifying questions. Afterward, you ask them to accept the team's goals and actively live the team's Work Agreements.

Oneness vs. Separateness

Oneness is a psychological state of mind. It can be described in many ways using phrases such as *None of us is as smart as all of us,* or *do no harm,* and *work as one.*

Separateness is the opposite of Oneness. To become a Right-Minded teammate, you must train your mind to choose attitudes and behaviors that create and extend Oneness, not project separateness.

For a list of 30 examples of Oneness, see the Right-Minded Teamwork Attitudes & Behaviors list found in numerous RMT books.

The concepts and story behind Oneness and separateness are introduced in RMT's book, **Reason, Ego & the Right-Minded Teamwork Myth:** *The Philosophy and Process for Creating a Right-Minded Team That Works Together as One.*

In this book, you will learn about Ego's "tiny, mad idea" of wanting more "stuff" and how Ego's choices led us all into a world of separation. That tiny, mad moment was, literally, the **birth of separation**. But, as the Myth reveals, Reason is always ready to lead us back into Oneness - our pre-separation state – joyfully described as the Unified Circle of Right-Minded Thinking where we can do no harm and work as one.

Preventions & Interventions

In RMT's ***Design a Right-Minded, Team-Building Workshop****: 12 Steps to Create a Team That Works as One*, the team-building facilitator and team leader meet early on to proactively identify potential issues that could keep teammates from achieving the workshop's desired outcomes.

This discussion leads to creating *preventions* that the team leader or facilitator takes to help prevent those issues from happening. The facilitator and team leader also agree on how to intervene in case the preventions don't work. Much of the time, however, preventions do their job and make *interventions* during team-building workshops unnecessary.

To learn more about effective preventions and interventions, go to RightMindedTeamwork.com or your favorite book retailer, and pick up your copy of these two books:

How to Facilitate Team Work Agreements: *A Practical, 10-Step Process for Building a Right-Minded Team That Works as One*

Design a Right-Minded, Team-Building Workshop: *12 Steps to Create a Team That Works as One*

Psychological Goals

A team's psychological goals describe how teammates intentionally choose to think and behave as they work together to achieve their team's business goals.

Psychological goals, such as achieving mutual trust and respect among teammates, may be viewed as a team's collective school of thought, values, or thought system.

These consciously chosen goals, captured in team Work Agreements, clarify the team's principles or standards of behavior.

Here is a specific example of a psychological goal you will find in several RMT materials:

> *When difficult team situations happen, we accept, forgive, and adjust our attitudes and behavior. We always find solutions because we believe that none of us is as smart as all of us.*

Reason

Reason is a mythological character and symbolic guide who shows you how to think and behave in a Right-Minded way. As your Right-Minded teacher, Reason helps you differentiate and choose between Right-Minded and wrong-minded attitudes and behaviors.

Reason is the opposite of Ego. Whereas Ego believes everyone is out to get you and instructs you to *do unto others before they do unto you,* Reason teaches you to *do unto others as you would have them do unto you.*

Ego encourages and projects separateness.
Reason cultivates and extends Oneness.

Reason is that part of your mind that always speaks for the Right Choice attitudes and behaviors. When you need a **moment of Reason** to find the best way to respond to a difficult team situation, say to yourself:

> *I am here to be truly helpful.*
>
> *I am here to represent Reason who sent me.*
>
> *I do not have to worry about what to say or what to do because Reason who sent me will direct me.*

When you experience a moment of Reason (a moment of revelation, clarity, or sanity regarding a particular challenge), "remembering" Reason's gentle guidance towards Oneness restores your mind to the forgiving Unified Circle of Right-Minded Thinking.

For the full story of Ego's tiny, mad idea of separation and how Reason waits even today to bring us back to Oneness, pick up the book *Reason, Ego & the Right-Minded Teamwork Myth: The Philosophy and Process for Creating a Right-Minded Team That Works Together as One*.

Reason, Ego & the Right-Minded Teamwork Myth

This book teaches two significant concepts:

- the Right-Minded Teamwork Myth is a short tale that presents RMT's underlying teamwork philosophy of doing no harm and working as one
- the Right-Minded Teamwork team-building tools, methods, and processes to create Right-Minded, productive teams.

The RMT Myth is a short, simple story. It follows three characters: Reason, Ego, and you, the Decision-Maker. Simply put, the RMT Myth and philosophy advocate for teammates to follow Reason's path of Oneness instead of following Ego's disastrous advice to seek separateness and prioritize selfishness.

Following the RMT Myth, you will learn about the Right-Minded Teamwork process. Unlike the story, the RMT process is no myth. It is practical, deliberate, and reliable.

The RMT process is a set of interconnected, team-building methods that together form a self-perpetuating, continuous improvement system. This process allows you to integrate the aspirations of the RMT Myth into your team in a way that helps you achieve your business goals.

This book teaches the RMT process and provides a clear overview of the seven other RMT team-building books that, when used together, form a continuous improvement process guaranteed to support team growth and success.

Recognition: Make It Easy to Keep Going

Authentic recognition is not about bestowing company shirts and prizes. It is about giving and receiving genuine appreciation for a job well done.

Recognition plays a critical role in growing your team's business because it keeps your team's spirit ignited. Unfortunately, many people work in team environments where there is little to no recognition. These teammates are discouraged. They do not give their best to the team. Why should they?

Discouraged teammates are like racehorses. If a horse is giving you only 80%, you can whip him, and he will give you 90%. Whip him again, and he will give you 100%. But if you whip him again, after he has already given you everything he has, he will drop back to 80%, or maybe even less. He has learned that you are going to whip him regardless, even if he works harder. So why should he give you his best?

Whipped people leave teams.

Far too often, the ones who leave are the most talented teammates. People that receive legitimate and genuine recognition stay and contribute. Shirts and prizes cannot earn that kind of loyalty or effort.

In the book ***Right-Minded Teamwork***: *9 Right Choices for Building a Team That Works as One*, you will learn that Recognition is one of the 9 Right Choices.

See **Critical Few: Complete Important Tasks First** for a related concept.

Right Choice Model

The *Right Choice Model* is an effective teaching aid that will help you and your teammates choose your own set of unique, "right" teamwork attitudes and behaviors.

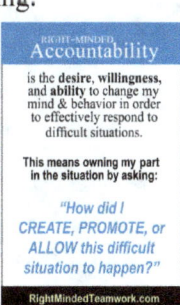

Inspired by *A Course in Miracles*, *The Right Choice Model* consists of two circles. The upper loop of acceptance, forgiveness, and adjustment represents the Unified Circle of Right-Minded Thinking.

The lower loop of rejection, Ego attack, and defensiveness describes the separated or divided circle of wrong-minded thinking.

To learn more about this simple but powerful teaching model, go to RightMindedTeamwork.com or your favorite book retailer, and pick up your copy of ***How to Apply the Right Choice Model***: *Create a Right-Minded Team That Works as One*.

Right-Minded Teamwork's 5-Element Framework

Right-Minded Teamwork is a business-oriented, psychological approach to team building where acceptance, forgiveness, and adjustment are teammate characteristics, and 100% customer satisfaction is the team's result.

Right-Minded Teamwork is built off a framework of 5 Elements consisting of two goals and three teamwork methods.

1. Team **Business Goal**: Achieve 100% Customer Satisfaction
2. Team **Psychological Goal**: Commit to Right-Minded Thinking
3. Team **Work Agreements**: Create & Follow Commitments
4. **Team Operating System**: Make It Effective & Efficient
5. **Right-Minded Teammates**: Strengthen Individual Performance

To learn more, go to RightMindedTeamwork.com or your favorite book retailer, and pick up your copy of ***Right-Minded Teamwork in Any Team***: *The Ultimate Team-Building Method to Create a Team That Works as One*.

Right-Minded Teamwork's 5 Element Implementation Plan

There is no one right way to implement RMT's 5 Elements but the three-workshop plan presented in the book ***Right-Minded Teamwork in Any Team***: *The Ultimate Team-Building Method to Create a Team That Works as One* has proven effective countless times.

Here's a brief overview.

First Workshop
Create **psychological goals** plus at least one **Work Agreement**.

Second Workshop
Reaffirm **business goals** and agree on a **team operating system**.

Third Workshop
Encourage and support Right-Minded **Teammate development**.

After the third workshop, and every 90 days after that, you will apply RMT's ***Team Operating System & Performance Factor Assessment*** to identify opportunities, take action, and achieve new teamwork improvements.

Right-Minded Teamwork Attitudes & Behaviors

The Right-Minded Teamwork model includes a list of 30 behavioral and process-oriented teammate attitudes and behaviors with their associated costs and benefits. I collected and compiled these over three decades of team-building workshops.

This valuable list includes clear, specific, right, and wrong behaviors "taught" to us by either Reason or Ego.

Thoughts and attitudes always precede teamwork behavior. Right-Minded attitudes come from Reason. Wrong-minded attitudes come from Ego.

The good news is that Right-Minded attitudes are natural. They are already inside you and your teammates. When you think about any of the wrong-minded Ego attitudes listed you will see in the list, ask yourself,

> *Was I born with these depressing, debilitating, and awful attitudes?*

Your answer will always be **"no!"** You learned those wrong-minded attitudes from Ego. That means *you can unlearn them, too*.

You can find the list in several RMT books, including ***How to Apply the Right Choice Model****: Create a Right-Minded Team That Works as One*, available at RightMindedTeamwork.com or your favorite book retailer.

Right-Mindedness vs. Wrong-Mindedness

"Mindedness" is what you choose to think and perceive. Right-Mindedness refers to the positive mental state, perceptions, choices, and actions you demonstrate when following Reason's guidance.

Wrong-mindedness refers to the negative mental state that occurs when you follow Ego's advice.

*Mindfulness is a journey without distance to a goal **you want to achieve**.*

In the book ***How to Apply the Right Choice Model***: *Create a Right-Minded Team That Works as One*, you will find a list of rewards and consequences for choosing Right-Mindedness.

In the book ***7 Mindfulness Training Lessons***: *Improve Teammates' Ability to Work as One with Right-Minded Thinking*, you will learn that in every circumstance, and especially during difficult team situations, Right-Minded Teammates practice mindfulness, or Right-Mindedness, to move them into an ally-focused way of thinking and behaving.

Both of these books will help you accept that your mind is split between two thought systems. At one moment, you are following Reason, and the next, Ego. It is impossible to create and sustain Right-Minded Thinking with a split mind. To heal your split mind, you want to apply the *7 Mindful Training Lessons* and the *Right Choice Model's* attitudes and behaviors.

To bring your team back into the forgiving Unified Circle of Right-Minded Thinking, pick up your copy of these books at your favorite book retailer or RightMindedTeamwork.com.

RMT Facilitator

The RMT Facilitator has a special function. Simply put, their expert facilitation *transforms* well-meaning dysfunctional souls into *healthy and functional teammates*.

Using the array of RMT tools, the RMT Facilitator guides teammates in converting their team mistakes into *do-no-harm-work-as-one* attitudes and behaviors.

Teammates are perpetually grateful for the RMT facilitator's help in achieving and sustaining Right-Minded Teamwork. Some even say their RMT Facilitator *saved them*. Team leaders and teammates continually seek the RMT Facilitator's support for years to come.

Team transformations are the RMT Facilitator's **special function**.

Team Management System:
An RMT Enterprise-Wide Process

An enterprise's Team Management System (TMS) aligns all teammates' attitudes and work behavior throughout the organization. An effective TMS ensures everyone is doing their part to help the organization achieve the enterprise's vision, mission, and strategic goals.

RMT's Team Management System involves integrating RMT's 5-Element Framework into all teams.

1. Team **Business Goal**: Achieve 100% Customer Satisfaction
2. Team **Psychological Goal**: Commit to Right-Minded Thinking
3. Team **Work Agreements**: Create & Follow Commitments
4. **Team Operating System**: Make It Effective & Efficient
5. **Right-Minded Teammates**: Strengthen Individual Performance

To learn more, go to RightMindedTeamwork.com or your favorite book retailer, and purchase your copy of *Achieve Your Organization's Strategic Plan: Create a Right-Minded, Team Management System to Ensure All Teams Work as One.*

Team Operating System & Performance Factor Assessment

RMT's Team Operating System is a six-step, 90-day, continuous improvement operating system that organizes your team functions to increase the likelihood of achieving customer satisfaction.

The system also includes the *Team Performance Factor Assessment* [step 3], which you will use to help teammates identify two to three improvement opportunities every 90 days.

The 25 performance factors in this assessment are aligned with and thus measure the six steps of RMT's Team Operating System. They effectively measure all aspects of Right-Minded Teamwork.

If you want your team to operate more effectively and efficiently, apply this 90-day process after your team has completed the first three RMT workshops. For a brief explanation, see the glossary: *Right-Minded Teamwork's 5 Element Implementation Plan.*

Apply the three-workshop plan and the operating system, and you nearly guarantee your team will create Right-Minded Teamwork.

To learn the process, go to RightMindedTeamwork.com or your favorite book retailer, and pick up your copy of **Right-Minded Teamwork in Any Team:** *The Ultimate Team-Building Method to Create a Team That Works as One.*

Thought System

<u>What you believe *is* your thought system</u>. Pause and reflect on this truth, and above all, be thankful that it is true.

Whether you are consciously aware of it or not, your thought system is the lens through which you view the world. Without exception, everyone has one. And though there are many variations, there are ***only two thought systems*** from which to choose:

- A Right-Minded thought system, which extends ally beliefs of acceptance, forgiveness, and adjustment to everyone, everywhere, forever
- A wrong-minded system, which projects adversarial assaults of rejection, attack, and defensiveness to everyone, everywhere, forever

Once you have developed a thought system of any kind, you live it and teach it. Even if you are not entirely aware of it, it remains at the forefront of your mind, influencing your daily behaviors and choices.

If your thought system is negative, or you choose to follow Ego into an unnecessary and adversarial competition, you cannot be a happy, successful teammate.

To live in the land of Oneness where your workplace is a safe and supportive classroom and where you and your teammates work as one to achieve team goals, you must train your mind and align your thought system with the teachings of Reason.

There is no possible compromise between these two thought systems. You either collaborate, or you compete. When you follow Ego, you take your team to the battleground. When you choose to follow Reason, you willingly create and genuinely strive to live your team's Work Agreements. With Reason's help, you transform your team into a lovely, collaborative, successful classroom.

The choice is clear.

Reject Ego. Embrace Reason.

Be Thankful.

Train Your Mind

When your mind is well-trained in Reason's Decision-Making ways, Ego attacks do not throw you off course. When a difficult team situation happens, you immediately stop for a **moment of Reason**. You refocus on Oneness, rise above the battleground, and remember to live your Work Agreements in your classroom.

To train your mind simply means practicing your team's Work Agreements, which represent your psychological goals, as often as possible, especially during difficult team situations.

Uncovering Root Cause

The Right-Minded Teamwork philosophy advocates leaders, teammates, and facilitators resolve the root cause of teamwork issues instead of making the mistake of addressing symptoms.

Though this view is discussed in many RMT materials, uncovering the root cause is heavily emphasized as a core concept in the book *Design a Right-Minded, Team-Building Workshop: 12 Steps to Create a Team That Works as One*.

Inside that book, you will find a story about a well-meaning team leader who asked me, as their team-building facilitator, if I could teach a three-day workshop in just two days. He believed a quick team event would address the problem he saw in his team.

But the problem he was seeing was only the symptom, not the root cause of the issue. Had I agreed and given him what he asked for, the team would still be struggling with the same issue. And, as a facilitator, I would have failed both the team and the leader.

Instead, by pausing to look for the root cause of the team challenge first, we ended up designing and executing a practical, Right-Minded Teamwork workshop to solve the actual underlying problem.

By seeking out the root cause first, we delivered the leader's desired result, even though the workshop we held was not what he had initially asked for.

To improve your ability to uncover root causes and read this short story, go to your favorite book retailer or RightMindedTeamwork.com and pick up your copy of *Design a Right-Minded, Team-Building Workshop: 12 Steps to Create a Team That Works as One*.

Unified Circle of Right-Minded Thinking

When your team discusses and agrees on your psychological goals – your consciously chosen set of attitudes and behaviors as described in your Work Agreements – you have created your team's collective thought system.

By uniting with each other in this way and openly committing to one another through your Work Agreements, you are renouncing Ego in yourself and your teammates and collectively committing to train your minds to follow Reason.

This process of creating team Work Agreements is your undivided declaration of interdependence. Your assertion is saying,

> *We hold these mindful truths to be self-evident that all minds are created equal, and whosoever believes that will have everlasting freedom to choose Right-Minded Teamwork.*

Your declaration plus your daily acts of living your team Work Agreements ***is your return*** to the forgiving Unified Circle of Right-Minded Thinking.

Work Agreements

A Work Agreement is a collective promise made by teammates to transform non-productive, adversarial behavior into collaborative teamwork behavior. Work Agreements are a key tool for teammates and teams who aspire to do no harm and work as one.

Work Agreements are not flimsy ground rules. They are emotionally mature work performance commitments. Work Agreements announce your dedication to Oneness and demonstrate your inner belief that *none of us is as smart as all of us.*

Your team's collective Work Agreements also define your team's psychological goals and thought system. They ensure you conduct your day-to-day work from within your team's Unified Circle of Right-Minded Thinking.

To learn more about the power of Work Agreements and how to use them to transform your team, go to RightMindedTeamwork.com or your favorite book retailer, and pick up your copy of ***How to Facilitate Team Work Agreements****: A Practical, 10-Step Process for Building a Right-Minded Team That Works as One.*

The End

On behalf of **Reason** and all the **Right-Minded Teammate Decision-Makers**, we extend our best wishes to you and your teammates as you create another *Right-Minded Team that Works Together as One.*

www.ingramcontent.com/pod-product-compliance
Lightning Source LLC
Chambersburg PA
CBHW072020110526
44592CB00012B/1378